Axminster .

Discover Devon

www.maverickguide.co.uk

@maverick.guide

EDITOR & DESIGN

Gabriella Dyson

OUR TALENTED TEAM

Contributors: Rachael Brown, Lucy Shrimpton, Amy Fry

Sub Editor: Molly Dyson

Cover Photo: Kingsweir by Patrycja Stubbs

Photographers: Collette Dyson, Amy Fry

Special Thanks: Chris Dyson

GET IN TOUCH

Editorial: editor@maverickguide.co.uk

Advertise with us: partnerships@maverickguide.co.uk

INSTAGRAM

@maverick.guide

MAVERICKGUIDE.CO.UK

Maverick

/mav(ə)rik/ | NOUN

A person who thinks and acts
independently, often behaving
differently from the expected or
usual way.

Hello there!

I'm probably rather biased, but I think Devon is a very special place. It's my home county and for that I count myself very lucky. Its rolling green hills and shingled beaches are the backdrop to my weekends, and for every charming little village — complete with colourful bunting and church fêtes - there are plenty of coastal towns that will give the Algarve a run for its money. In this guide, we uncover some of Devon's hidden gems, as well as the talented artisans and unique experiences it has to offer. So, join us in tossing aside run-of-the-mill handbooks and embrace a whole new kind of travel...

Gabriella Dyson

Editor & Founder

Torquay Marina, Roberto La Rosa

24 hours in

The English Riviera

There's a reason why The English Rivera routinely tips the charts as the UK's most popular place to staycation. The region covers 22 miles of South Devon coastline, from Torquay to Berry Head, and is home to several award-winning beaches, exotic palm trees and quintessentially British towns...

Torbay has earned something of a bad rep in recent years, due in part to its claim to fame as the setting for John Cleese's Fawlty Towers. But if you know where to look, it's not all chain restaurants and seaside arcades...

Overlooking Torquay Marina you'll find **The Elephant Restaurant** (p.130) which offers Michelin Star dining with an affordable pricetag. In the sunshine, Torquay Marina is a lovely spot for a stroll and is a great starting point for sceneic coastal walks. Head to nearby **Meadfoot Beach** to follow in the footsteps of famed Torbay resident, Agatha Christie. The Queen of Crime once called this stretch of coastline home and set many of her novels in the area. Today, Meadfoot is a Blue Flag beach lined with colourful huts and a popular café.

Alternatively, you could shake off the touristy crowds and head to **Oddicombe Beach** for a refreshing dip in clear waters. Paddle boards and kayaks are available for hire and seals are often spotted around the bay. This unspoilt shingle beach is linked to **Babbacombe Bay** by a well-trodden beachside path, as well as by the Babbacombe Cliff Railway (a seriously nostalgic transport system that has shuttled hundreds of thousands visitors from A to B since it was built in 1926). Once you arrive at Babbacombe you can take a stroll at picturesque **Babbacombe Downs**, the highest cliff top promenade in all of England. On a clear day you can see right across to Portland Bill in Dorset.

A short drive from the coast will take you to the thatched cottages of Cockington. The centrepiece of this quaint countryside village is **Cockington Court**: a thriving community of artisans, including glassblowers, cider makers, chocolatiers, ateliers and bakers. Wander through the charming manor grounds and browse the handmade produce of local craftspeople.

We think **Brixham** is one of Devon's most photogenic towns, with its rainbow spectrum of buildings cascading down the hillside toward its harbour. At its heart, Brixham is very much a working fishing community, so expect to spy heritage trawlers hauling in their daily catch and tiny day boats zipping in and out of the marina.

No doubt the first thing you'll spot in Brixham is **The Golden Hind.** It's a full-sized replica of Sir Francis Drake's iconic ship of the same name and it's been a notable Brixham landmark since 1964. The ship has a long history of film and television appearances and is open to visitors as an interactive museum. Kids will have a swashbuckling time playing pirates on its deck and for the extra adventurous you can even spend a night onboard!

Pack your swimwear and get over to **Shoalstone Seawater Pool.** It's one of the last remaining sea water swimming pools in the UK and it occupies a stunning position on Brixham sea front. Local people took over management of the pool back in 2014, so the community spirit here is palpable. While you're there, don't miss **Shoals Restaurant.** This friendly eatery is the brainchild of a local Brixham fishing family, so expect the menus to be a tasty homage to the local coastline. Every table on their al fresco deck offers diners the best seat in the house, overlooking the lido and the glistening sea beyond.

MORE ENGLISH RIVIERA

Hotels
The Cary Arms Hotel & Spa, Torquay

Self-Catering Properties
Higher Lodge Cottage (Airbnb)
Faithful, Brixham Harbour

Camping & Glamping
Brownscombe Luxury Glamping

Shopping
ROAM by Drifting Bear Co, Teignmouth.

Cafés & Bistros
Margo's, Torquay
Wesup Coffee, Cocktails & Eatery, Torquay
The Curious Kitchen, Brixham

Restaurants & Bars
Rockfish, Brixham
The Ness, Teignmouth

Boringdon Hall
Hotel & Spa

Known as the 'enchanted place on the hill', Boringdon Hall Hotel & Spa offers a truly exceptional experience from the moment you step through the door. From its luxe four-poster bedrooms to its fine dining restaurant and award-winning spa, this 16th-century manor house hotel has it all. Boringdon Hall is conveniently located between Plymouth and Dartmoor, making it the perfect backdrop for romantic weekend getaways and relaxing staycations. Step out onto the perfectly kept lawn that overlooks the manor, breathe in the fresh country air and take in the rolling Devonshire hills. These magnificent views alone almost guarantee a five-star escape but it's the hotel's flawless facilities that will seal the deal...

Rooms at Boringdon Hall are historic and sophisticated, offering period features alongside contemporary luxury. Many rooms boast four-poster beds and heavy wooden beams that hint of the manor's vibrant past. We're willing to wager that

Boringdon Hall is the only place in the world where you can soak away your stresses in a jacuzzi that's housed within the original turret of an Elizabethan manor. At the heart of the hotel sits its exquisite Great Hall, which serves as the bar and lounge. This impressive, wood-panelled room is dominated by an enormous stone fireplace, above which sits the coat of arms of King James I (just one of many indications of the manor's illustrious royal connections). If period dramas are your thing, you're in luck. The hotel has a fascinating history and it's previous owners read like a who's who of the royal court.

Overlooking the Great Hall is Àclèaf Restaurant, which is an absolute must for anyone who appreciates good food. This fine dining restaurant oozes sophistication and Head Chef Scott Paton's signature dishes showcase inventive British fare, using the finest Devon ingredients. As testament to

Àclèaf's gourmet credentials it has been awarded 4 AA Rosettes and has been featured in the coveted Michelin Guide. Menus are crafted around sumptuous seasonal ingredients like crab, wagyu, tarragon and marrow, and there's always a delightful vegan dish on offer. Ask for a wine reccomendation to complement your meal or order a G&T made with Boringdon Hall's very own gin, distilled onsite.

For the curious amongst you, try and find the secret bar, furnished in dark velvet and complete with antique books and glowing fireplace. It's the perfect hidden corner for a secret after-dinner drink.

A stay at Boringdon Hall wouldn't be complete without making the most of its £5 million state-of-the-art Gaia Spa. This exclusively adult retreat offers an extensive range of nourishing treatments and therapeutic rituals, using both hot and cool water and sumptuous Gaia skincare products (read more on p.136). Start to unwind in the hydrotherapy swimming pool – it's heated to a perfect 30 degrees – and let the waterfalls massage the tension out of your shoulders and neck. The pool extends outside, which is wondrous when the sun is shining and you can enjoy views of the wild Dartmoor

countryside from the water. Keep the relaxation going with a detox in the traditional steam room or discover the soothing benefits of the Crystal Salt steam room. Spa treatments vary from massages to facials, holistic treatments and relaxing sessions in the Laconium herbal sauna. There's also a cluster of alfresco jacuzzis outside on the patio that are available to book ahead of time. Outside the pool you can relax on the decking or take a seat at one of the 'Spatisserie' outdoor tables for a healthy brunch or a small bite to eat.

Hotel Address:
Boringdon Hall Hotel, Colebrook, Plymouth, Devon PL7 4DP

Maverick Tip:
Rooms are available from 3pm but if you arrive early you can make use of the Gaia Spa facilities from 12pm or book one of Boringdon's hugely popular afternoon teas.

Find Boringdon Hall online:
boringdonhall.co.uk
@boringdonhall

Smeatons Tower, Amy Fry

visit

Plymouth

Curated by Amy Fry

The historic maritime city of Plymouth lines the picturesque
South West coastline of Devon and is home to the iconic
Smeaton's Tower, the original 1935 Art Deco Lido and the
Plymouth Gin Distillery. Often undervalued in its appeal,
Plymouth has its fair share of hidden gems and stunning
vistas that are not to be missed. With the sandy beaches of
the South Hams coastline to the right, the entrance into
Cornwall to the left and the sweeping moorland of Dartmoor
National Park above, its location is a tough one to beat.

A trip to the **Royal William Yard** should be at the top of your itinerary when visiting the Ocean City. The historic Grade I-listed military buildings now play host to an abundance of eateries, shops, outdoor activities and markets. Such markets include **Native Makers**; an independent platform for creatives to showcase their craft and tempt you into buying a gift or two. Check the Royal William Yard website for market days so you don't miss out.

For the adventurous, **South West SUP** offers paddle-board lessons and board hire. Bespoke classes are available for individuals and groups, and we recommend checking out their sunset and full moon paddle sessions.

A new addition to Plymouth is **The Alma Yard**, a mini hub of creative minds, studio spaces, cafés and bakeries. One studio, in particular, is home to Megan of Flotsam Prints, exhibiting a beautiful array of hand-crafted lino prints inspired by her sea swimming pursuits.

The Hutong Café is Plymouth's original bagel house offering delicious meat, veggie and vegan fillings. Located just outside the entrance to the Royal William Yard, be sure to stop by and grab yourself a coffee and a bite to eat.

Immerse yourself into houseplant heaven by visiting **Nook Houseplants** and discover a new leafy companion within their selection of both rare and common houseplants. They also stock a variety of clay, ceramic, concrete and seagrass plant pots from local makers.

If you're after a treat or two, head down to **Jacka Bakery** situated on Plymouth's historic Barbican. Everything they sell is freshly baked from scratch that day including an array of sweet and savoury favourites and hearty sourdough bread.

When in Plymouth, you would be a fool not to head into **The Harbour** to taste the Plymouth-caught fish and chips. The seafood restaurant is at arms-length from the seafront where you can gaze upon the colourful fishing boats and cobbled streets of the Barbican.

With views spanning the charming Plymouth Sound, the **Ocean View** restaurant has one of the best dining outlooks that Plymouth has to offer. Not only is the view so great, but the interior has been tastefully designed with an Art Deco theme running throughout. The original glass dome roof provides an amphitheatre for the bar area uniquely located in the centre of the restaurant.

In 2020 Plymouth's former Museum and Central Library were transformed into a series of state-of-the-art galleries and exhibition spaces known as **The Box.** Head here to soak up some culture and discover exhibitions from UK leading artists. Stay for **The Box Kitchen & Bar,** where you can dine under a fleet of floating figureheads, whose carved faces used to glide across the ocean on the bows of Plymouth ships.

Sushi lovers ought to pay a visit to **KuKu**; an elegant yet modern Japanese restaurant that brings together vibrant colours and delicate flavours.
The ingredients are both local and seasonal mixed with traditional Japanese offerings which provide you with an exquisite dining experience.

Find **Custom House Cellar Bar** hidden in the heart of the Barbican. Just head down the stairs of the Grade II-listed building and you will find yourself in medieval times where candelabras and exposed brickwork are met with some of the finest cocktails in the city.

MORE PLYMOUTH

Cafés & Bistros
Cosmic Kitchen
Boston Tea Party
Rhubarb & Mustard

Restaurants & Bars
Barbican Kitchen
The Hook and Line
The Fig Tree @ 36
Le Vignoble
Honky Tonk Wine Library

Shopping
Domea Favour
Identity Fashion
Minerva

Galleries
HOST Galleries
45 Southside Gallery
The Arts Institute

Experiences
The Plymouth Gin Distillery
Barbican Theatre
Ocean Markets

Maverick loves

Gara Rock

Perched on the South West Coast Path high above rugged coves, you'll find Gara Rock. This boutique hotel and spa is undoubtedly one of Devon's coolest destinations and boasts some of the best coastal vistas in all of England. With its sensational setting, stylish interiors and delectable food it's easy to see why Gara Rock has earned a glowing reputation among discerning travellers. Here's why we think it should be top of your list when booking a trip to Devon...

A chic, coastal aesthetic runs throughout each of Gara Rock's beautifully styled rooms and suites. Expect plenty of sumptuous velvets, rustic timber-clad walls, geometric tiles and subtle nods to the nautical. There's luxury to be found in every corner, from spacious balconies and garden terraces to bespoke argan oil toiletries. What's more, thanks to Gara Rock's enviable clifftop position, most of its accommodation enjoys sea views.

Travelling as a group? Opt for something out of the ordinary and book a stay in Signal House: a gorgeous two bedroom retreat for four. Unwind with friends in the bubbling hot tub or throw open the doors to enjoy drinks on your very own sun terrace. For those in pursuit of something extra special, look no further than The Secret Suite. Nestled on the clifftop, away from the main hotel, this romantic bolthole offers endless sea views and a handful of friendly sheep for company. Lose time unwinding in the roll-top bath, take a sunset dip in the hot tub or curl up with a bottle of fizz in the glass-fronted living room.

Wherever you choose to lay your head, be sure to make the most of everything else on offer There's a host of ways to achieve your very own nirvana, whether it's lazy laps in one of the two pools or catching a movie in the 12-seater cinema room (armed with plenty of snacks, of course).

Press pause, relax and unwind at Wild Rock Spa. There's a menu of restorative treatments on offer, as well as manicures, pedicures and body scrubs to indulge in. We suggest steaming away your stresses in the sauna or soaking up the sea views in the jacuzzi. Gara Rock likes to keep things local, which is why they use Apothespa skincare products at Wild Rock Spa. They're organic, natural and vegan and they're handmade in the colourful town of Totnes just down the road from the hotel.

One of Gara Rock's most impressive features is its main restaurant. Floor-to-ceiling glass walls look out over the sea, so you can watch the waves rolling in as you enjoy a menu of seasonal, bistro-style food. Herbs and fresh salad leaves are plucked fresh from the kitchen garden, while flowering rosemary is foraged from the nearby cliffs. Expect everything else to be sourced from local producers, meaning you'll experience an authentic taste of Devon during your visit.

The Ox Grill is Gara Rock's answer to al fresco dining. Sit on the landscaped terrace as chefs whip up tantalising dishes over glowing embers. Mixing land, sea and allotment, there are plenty of tempting dishes to try while you breathe in the fresh coastal air. Round off the evening with a nightcap in the stylish Lounge Bar, cosying up in an armchair or melting into a sofa with a drink in hand. There's a range of vintages, homemade cordials and cocktails on the drinks list, but you really ought to sample Gara Rock's very own gin.

Hotel Address:
East Portlemouth, Near Salcombe
South Devon, TQ8 8FA

Maverick Tip:
Book a private slot in the cinema room to have the place to yourself. You can even bring your favourite DVD along to watch on the big screen.

Find Gara Rock online:
www.gararock.com
@gararockhotel

24 hours in

Salcombe

Salcombe is a real gem of a town, where luxury yachts bob on calm turquoise waters and the streets are lined with pastel-hued boutiques and galleries. It's home to a well-heeled crowd and acts like a magnet to discerning Londoners, who flock to the town each summer to enjoy its pristine sandy beaches and its vibrant boating community...

Start your visit on Island Street, the artisanal heart of Salcombe. Here you'll find freshly hauled lobster and crab for sale, alongside traditional boatbuilders and shops selling seaside paraphernalia. While you're there, sample a cone of delicious **Salcombe Dairy Ice Cream.** Their flavours range from strawberries & cream to decadent banoffee and a curiously named 'Salcombe mud' (which is really just a tasty chocolate, shortbread combo).

Salcombe punches well above its size when it comes to retail therapy. This small estuary town is the birthplace of big brands like **Jack Wills**, **Crew Clothing** and **Quba Sails.** On its vibrant Fore Street you'll find shops selling everything from designer fashion to artisan food, stylish homewares and seaside essentials. **Chattels Of Salcombe** at 11 Fore Street are purveyors of consciously sourced and beautifully designed homewares. **Cranch's Sweetshop** is the stuff of Salcombe legend. It first opened its doors at 78 Fore Street back in 1869 and it honestly hasn't changed a great deal over the years. Its candy pink facade and nostalgic treats will no doubt tempt children and the young at heart through its doors.

There's something about the waft of salt on the clean air in Salcombe that makes you crave a crisp G&T. If you can find a coveted slot, book a date at **Salcombe Distilling Co.'s Gin School** where you can develop and distil your very own 70cl blend of gin. Afterward we suggest kicking back in their waterside bar and taking in the beautiful creek views with a chilled drink in hand.

Locals love **The Crab Shed** restaurant. Situated right on the waters edge (head along Gould Road) their seafood-focussed menu makes great use of the fresh ingredients landed right on their doorstep – and by 'ingredients' we're largely referring to Salcombe crab. You can order potted crab, crab bisque, crab sarnies, and even crab bouillabaisse. Not enough crustacean on your plate? Order the 'Shed Crab Fries' for a portion of crispy chips topped with fresh crabmeat, chilli, parmesan, spring onions and coriander. De-licious.

From the centre of Salcombe, stroll along along Cliff Road for about 15 minutes and you'll arrive at **North Sands Beach.** This large sandy beach is perfect for families and welcomes dogs year round. From its golden shores you can enjoy stunning views of the Kingsbridge Estuary. While you're there, grab a bite to eat across the road at **The Winking Prawn Beach Café.** This Salcombe institution has been welcoming diners for over 20 years with its own particular brand of shabby chic beach décor. Thanks to its close proximity to the beach, you can sit in the sunshine and graze on platters of fresh shellfish or buckets of juicy prawns.

Mill Bay Beach is a just a quick ferry ride across the water from Salcombe. It's a glorious little sandy beach that's warmed by the sun throughout the day. Low tide reveals a wealth of rock pools to explore and the calm waters make it perfect for swimming. From Mill Bay car park you can also cut through the woods and arrive at **Sunny Cove Beach** within a few minutes. On an evening, Sunny Cove is a great spot from which to watch the sun go down – just don't get caught by the tide.

Speaking of tides, when it's high tide you can cruise up the water to reach **Millbrook Inn.** This hidden foodie gem is nestled at the top of a tranquil tidal creek and for generations it has held a special place in the hearts of locals and honorary locals alike. Situated right on the water, you'll arrive for the stunning location and stay for its quality Devonshire pub fayre.

Salcombe Harbour Hotel

Merchants House

MORE SALCOMBE PICKS:

Self-Catering Properties
Merchants House & The Booty
Pitchford House (Airbnb)
Brightham House Boutique B&B

Hotels
Salcombe Harbour Hotel

Cafés & Bistros
Sailor V
Salcombe Coffee Company
The Pantry Coffee House
Bo's Beach Café
The Blue Whale Café

Restaurants & Bars
The Fortescue Inn
Dick and Willis
The Ferry Inn

Food & Drink Shops
Bowers Wines & Spirits
Roly's Fudge Pantry
The Salcombe Deli

Clothing Boutiques
Maxari
Salcombe Clothing Company
Amelia's Attic
Busby & Fox
Love from Luella

Homewares & Lifestyle
Salcombe Antiques
Mo Logan Antiques
Susie Watson Designs
Paper Bird Island
Tinc

Galleries
Gallery 5
Love the Sea Gallery
Drang Gallery
The Tonic Gallery
Rowbury

Experiences
Sea Kayak Salcombe

Maberly House

salcombe

Maberly House is the perfect luxury holiday home for spending time with family and friends. This elegant Georgian farmhouse sits in its own secluded grounds in the stunning countryside of south Devon, just a short drive from many perfect beaches.

Lovingly styled to create a comfortable, relaxed and memorable experience, the house boasts seven beautiful bedrooms, five bathrooms, plus two stylish sitting rooms, and a large dining room. The downstairs space features many sumptuous sofas and two wood-burning stoves for cosy evenings spent by the fire. There's also a large kitchen with farmhouse table and French doors that lead out to a sheltered outdoor dining space. The acre of land surrounding Maberly House is there to be explored, so help yourself to the apples growing in the orchard, host a croquet match on the lawn, and finish the day off with a barbecue in the sunshine.

Maverick tip: The House is surrounded by fantastic walks with plenty of worthy food stops. Combine the breathtaking coastline of East Prawle with a drink at The Pig's Nose or work up an appetite walking the headland around Mill Bay, before whipping up your own roast dinner to enjoy in Maberly's historic 16th-century dining room.

Book via salcombefinest.com

Hope Cove House

inner hope

Hope Cove House is an inviting family-run hotel with
stylish and arty interiors on the South Devon coast.
Overlooking the bay of Inner Hope - nestled between
Salcombe to the South and Thurlestone to the North - few
venues are as idyllically located as this.
A theme of white walls and picture windows runs
throughout this bijou hotel, with vibrant pops of colour
introduced via textiles, with light, airy bedrooms offering
views of the gorgeous sandy bay beyond.

The restaurant serves dishes that are seasonal and
coastal, and Hope Cove House is also partial to holding
summer barbecues on their upper terrace. So, you can fall
asleep with a full belly and listen to the sound of waves
lapping in and out of the cove. Bliss.

Maverick Tip: The sitting room, bar and restaurant are
open plan. If you would rather not be surrounded by lego
or sticky fingers, book outside of school holidays!

hopecovehouse.co

Kingsweir, Patrycja Stubbs

discover

The South Hams

Much of The South Hams is designated as an
Area of Outstanding Natural Beauty and its stunning
landscape, with all its rivers and rias, coves and
creeks, has plenty to appreciate and explore.
Amongst the rolling green hills and blue coastal
towns, there are exciting pockets of artisan
producers, independent shops and passionate
makers to discover...

If you're willing to set aside a day for wild swimming, pootle down the estuary on **South Devon's River Avon** and let the current gently carry you down to sandy **Bantham Beach**. There's a car park in Aveton Gifford – start here and slide into the river. Enjoy its steady pull as you drift downstream, floating on your back as the landscape passes by you. The sandy riverbed makes for clear waters and a soft ground underfoot. Wearing a wetsuit and boots is best for the walk back, and it goes without saying that you should always consult the tide times before setting off and make sure someone on dry land knows what you're doing.

When you arrive at Bantham Beach why not brush up on your surfing, SUP, or kayaking on its pristine sands? South Devon's most renowned surf spot. Qualified instructors from **Bantham Surfing Academy** can offer guidance – and patience – taking you up the River Avon on a paddleboard or improving your surfing in a couple of hours. Otherwise, there are boards for hire on the beach. For something a little different, one of their adventure kayak tours will take you to Burgh Island and its snorkelling coves.

Burgh Island is a private, secluded tidal island that's home to famed Art Deco hotel built in 1929. **Burgh Island Hotel** still boasts many of its original interiors and has a fascinating history sprinkled with tales of legendary guests. Adding to the 'Great Gatsby' vibe is its impressive Grand Ballroom, where tasting menus are accompanied by live piano music and black tie is encouraged. Next to the hotel you'll find **The Pilchard Inn**: a weather-beaten smugglers inn with over 700 years of history. Find a cosy corner by an open fire and sample a host of locally brewed craft beers, wines and local ciders.

No visit to the South Hams would be complete without a trip to the enchanting waterside town of **Dartmouth**. Its sweeping hillside is covered in candy coloured houses that lead down to the banks of the River Dart. A trek up to the top of **Jawbone Hill** offers a beautiful panoramic vista at the top, but it's worth taking a day to explore the town itself. Its ancient narrow streets are home to a myriad of boutique shops, delicatessens and art galleries.

Spend an afternoon milling in and out of colourful backstreet galleries (mostly selling affordable art and gifts geared toward tourists) or stroll along the embankment and watch the boats bobbing on the water.

Dartmouth's foodie credentials are top notch. To experience the best seafood in town book a table at **The Seahorse Restaurant.** It's an elegant bistro with leather banquettes, white tablecloths and flickering candles. Breathe in the intoxicating aromas of the open charcoal grill and finish off your evening with a bottle of Seahorse Rosé in adjoining **Joe's Bar**.

Head to **ANDRIA** for exquisitely presented Modern European cuisine. Head chef Luca Berardino was born in Paris and raised on five generations of Italian home cooking (so you just know his food is next level).

Bar 1620 is a sophisticated yet laidback venue that serves an excellent range of cocktails. Sit by the wood-burner and enjoy a drink in their 'cosy corner' or head over on a Thursday night for live music sessions.

You'll find that the best views of Dartmouth are from the water itself, so you could always hire a boat from **Dartmouth Boat Hire Company**. Their self-steer boats let you explore the River Dart at your own pace. Cruise along the water to the idyllic village of Dittisham, a popular spot for locals thanks to its unspoilt beauty and a sense that it operates outside of normal time. Sink a pint of traditional ale at the characterful **Ferry Boat Inn** (you won't miss its bright pink exterior) or feast on freshly caught crab at **The Anchor Stone Café.**

A short drive – or a brisk walk – from Dartmouth town centre gets you to **Dartmouth Castle.** The castle, which has origins dating back to 1388, is managed by English Heritage and allows its visitors to explore its ancient passageways and climb to the top of its turrets for unbeatable estuary views. Visit their onsite cafe to enjoy an authentic Devonshire cream tea in the sunshine and watch as sailing boats drift by.

Close to the castle is **Gallants Bower** – a medieval fort built during the English Civil War. In May, the whole area is carpeted by beautiful bluebells and is a truly idyllic spot for a stroll. Walk a little further along the coastline and you'll arrive at one of South Devon's most photogenic places: **Sugary Cove Beach**. It's largely hidden by woodland, so it's easy to miss – especially since there are no signs. Follow the steep rock steps down to this remote shingle beach and see if you can nab one of the three picnic benches. It's a lovely spot to picnic in the sun or take a dip in the water.

On a sunny day, **South Milton Sands** is glorious. It's perfectly positioned for the golden hour, catching the sun as it hazily sets over the glittering sea and iconic Thurlestone Rock. **The Beachhouse** is a foodie hotspot that soaks up these views and satisfies all seafood cravings in the process. Although it's a beachside café – and has all the relaxed vibes of one – the price tag is more akin to a typical restaurant. However, the food is so good we're sure you won't mind. Expect overflowing platters of freshly caught and simply cooked seafood, such as meaty crab claws and plump mussels.

Pleasantly full, head back to a darling self-catering property like **Bowcombe Boathouse** on the Kingsbridge Estuary. What was once the disused storage shed of a traditional Salcombe Yawl, has now been lovingly restored in dark teak and aged brass, and decorated with found and foraged materials. Curl up with a blanket on the decking and watch the ever-changing views of the estuary.

Bowcombe Boathouse by Alie Victoria

Dart Marina Hotel, Rachael Hoile

Bantham Beach by Jim Catlin /Shutterstock

MORE SOUTH HAMS

Self-Catering Properties

Harberton Manor

Golden Meadow, Widewell

Beam Ends, Beesands

Highview House, Dartmouth

The Pink House, Dartmouth

The Old Stables Apartment, Dartmouth

Camping & Glamping

Fountain Violet Farm, Kingswear

Hotels

Thurlestone Hotel, Thurlestone

The Whitehouse Boutique Hotel

Dart Marina Hotel, Dartmouth

Cafés & Bistros

Fika, Kingsbridge

The Curious Kitchen, Brixham

Flavel Café, Dartmouth

Clothing Boutiques

Coco Boutique, Kingsbridge

Starburst Boutique, Dartmouth

Eleven Clothing, Dartmouth

Restaurants & Bars

The Ship Inn, Noss Mayo

Lobster Pod Bistro, Hope Cove

The Venus Company, Blackpool Sands

The Cricket Inn, Beesands

The Pigs Nose Inn, East Prawle

Taylor's, Dartmouth

Chez Rosa, Dartmouth

Brewed Boy, Dartmouth

The Sail Loft, Dartmouth

The Bear & Blacksmith, Chillington

Food & Drink Shops

South Devon Chilli Farm, Loddiswell

Barrell & Still, Kingsbridge

The Deli at Dartmouth

Smith Street Deli, Dartmouth

Dartmouth Wine Company

Homewares & Lifestyle

Relish Lifestyle, Kingsbridge

The General Store, Kingsbridge

Classics Reclamation, Kingsbridge

The Barn Avon Mill, Loddiswell

Distinctly Living, Dartmouth

The Batman's Summerhouse

kingsbridge

No, not that Batman. This cosy cabin was once the 1930s summer house of a military gentleman rather than a caped crusader and is now a hidden gem filled with treasured keepsakes and locally made furniture. Sitting right on the riverbank, it blends into the scenic landscape but there is plenty to do on its doorstep.

Inside, the cabin's interiors have been inspired by family summerhouses in Scandinavia: fresh white walls and grey paintwork, solid wood floors and airy rooms, a personal collection of mid-century furniture and locally made one-offs. There's everything you could possibly need to relax and unwind. Sink into the sofa with a glass of wine or nap outside in the hammock when the sun is out.

Maverick tip: If cooking isn't on the agenda, head to The Sloop Inn, just down the road in Bantham.

instagram.com/batmanssummerhouse

The Shippon

Landscove

'Shippon' is a traditional Devonian word for a cattle barn and for the last few hundred years this gorgeous Airbnb wasn't much more than that. But after being lovingly converted by its talented owners, The Shippen in Landscove now offers its guests a calm and luxurious base from which to explore South Devon.

From its weathered oak ceilings to its hand-built kitchen and restored antique woodburner, The Shippon is a design lover's dream. This cosy bolthole features warmly-lit nooks and woollen blankets to cocoon yourself in. The king-size bed has been handmade from walnut and oak and the kitchen is fully equipped with everything you could need to whip up tasty meals. Open up the cupboards and you'll find locally-made bespoke black porcelain crockery and freshly ground coffee for lazy mornings. Grab yourself a book from the bookshelf and plonk yourself onto the impossibly soft feather sofa or head out to the private patio space to relax and unwind. Surrounded by ferns, flowers and a lily pond, it's a lovely sunspot and the perfect place to soak up the sunset with a glass of wine in hand...

Maverick tip: On request, the owners can stock the wine rack, prepare a breakfast hamper, or fill the fridge with local handcrafted beer for your arrival.

Bookable via Airbnb

Totnes, Philip Bird

visit

Totnes

The ancient market town of Totnes is renowned as a magnet for artists, 'alternative types' and London expats seeking the simplicity of rural life. Its colourful High Street is built into a steep hillside that threads its way upward from the River Dart. It's home to an eclectic range of independent shops, quirky cafés and galleries, as well as a thriving market scene.

At the base of the hill sits **The Curator Café.** It's no secret that these guys serve the best flat white in town. So grab yourself one of their speciality wood-roasted coffees and nibble on some handmade biscotti as you flick through their collection of vintage books and magazines. Upstairs – almost hidden – you'll find **The Curator Kitchen.** The menu here changes weekly but one thing remains consistent: Italian flavours are king. Expect fresh antipasti, delicious homemade pasta dishes and a variety of natural wines.

As you climb the hill, don't miss **Studio Nine** on the right. It's an ever-changing pop-up space conceived of by entrepreneur Lucie Cast. The studio gives local makers, designers and artists the rare opportunity to take over a prime retail space on a week-by-week basis. The results have been varied and exciting, with the studio hosting everything from up-and-coming fashion designers to art exhibitions. Elsewhere in town, **The Old Bakehouse** follows a similar ethos. Housed in a former bakery, the building features its original 1907 bread oven, as well as a gorgeous flagstone floor and beautifully-aged subway tiles. Today, it hosts a variety of foodie pop-up events within its historic walls.

Rumour Wine Bar is a popular spot that's usually packed with locals. It's housed in a 14th-century building that once served as a toffee factory and a jazz club (sadly not at the same time). The atmosphere is warm and the service is relaxed, but it's the food that keeps us coming back for more. Portions are seriously generous and their epic Sunday roasts take some beating.

Totnes Market Square is a thriving hub of activity. Every Friday and Saturday you can catch a busy market, with stalls selling food, clothes, plants and bric-a-brac. Friday is flea market day and if you arrive early enough you can often nab yourself an antique or some pre-loved furniture.

Overlooking Rotherfold Square is the gorgeous **Me & East** (pictured right). It's filled with all manner of beautiful things, from tactile ceramics to hand-poured candles, unique jewellery and bath oils. Basically, it's the sort of shop where you'll want to pick up and take everything home with you. Plus, it's all made by small UK businesses and independent craftspeople.

Totnes Castle, Tomas Marek

Me & East

The Bull Organic Inn is a beautifully restored pub with rooms that serves simple, organic dishes cooked from scratch. Upstairs features eight rooms with super comfy beds and eclectic handpicked furniture.

Managed by English Heritage, **Totnes Castle** is a classic motte and bailey castle, founded soon after the Norman conquest. Climb to the very top of the castle keep and enjoy the far-reaching views over Totnes town and across to the River Dart. On a summer's day we recommend bringing your own picnic to enjoy in the grounds under the shelter of its ancient trees.

Make the trip to **Sharpham Estate** to experience their award-winning vineyard and winery. Nestled in the beautiful Dart Valley, Sharpham's experienced team offer vineyard tours and guided cheese and wine tastings. Also onsite is **Circa at Sandridge Barton** – a charming restaurant showcasing produce from the estate and local suppliers.

Make sure **Nkuku** (pictured top left) is on your Totnes itinerary. This nationally acclaimed homeware brand has its roots in South Devon, where you can find their flagship store. It's brimming with beautiful homewares made using recycled materials and sustainable methods. At the heart of the shop you'll find its equally stylish Café, which beckons you in with the tempting aroma of wood-roasted coffee.

Riverford Field Kitchen ticks all the right boxes for us. Organic, plough-to-plate food is the name of the game, with an emphasis on dishes that elevate the humble vegetable. Menus change daily, depending on what's growing in the surrounding fields and polytunnels, and even the most committed carnivores will find themselves in awe of what these guys can do with their five-a-day.

The Bull Inn, Rachael Hoile

MORE TOTNES PICKS:

Self-Catering Properties
Wood Farm Devon
The Albatross
The Garden Flat (Airbnb)

Cafés & Bistros
The Hairy Barista
Mangetout
Waterside Bistro
Wild Thyme Deli & Kitchen
The Almond Thief, Dartington

Restaurants & Bars
Gather
Taguchi Ya
Royal Seven Stars
The Totnes Brewing Co
New Lion Brewery, Dartington

Food & Drink Shops
Ben's Farm Shop
The Happy Apple
Delphini's Gelato

Clothing Boutiques
Fifty5a
Butterworth's Vintage
Revival
Glow

Lifestyle & Gifts
Inspired Buys
Drift Record Shop
Holly Keeling Interiors
Devon Makers
Fox & Company
Forest & Co

Galleries
A Pickled Thought
The Bowie Gallery
White Space Art

Experiences
Dartington Estate
Totnes Cinema

The Lost Music Hall

nr Totnes

In a hidden South Hams valley you'll find an enchanting homestay known as 'The Lost Music Hall'. This unique country escape once served as a London Dandy's secret retreat from society. Today it welcomes you to make yourself at home in his music hall of enormous proportions.

Inside, The Lost Music Hall pays homage to the property's Arts and Crafts roots, with a pared-back period aesthetic. Oak parquet flooring gleams in the light-filled living spaces and auction finds sit in harmony with pieces imported from the owners' New York loft. Upstairs, spectacular valley views wrap around the balcony, and each bedroom generously boasts not one but two double beds.

The music hall and adjoining manor sit in over seven acres of Devonshire countryside, shaded by ancient trees and crossed by the gurgling Ambrook river (perfect for a cool dip on a balmy afternoon). You'll have private use of the games room, terraces and back garden during your stay, as well as the heated outdoor swimming pool (May-September).

Maverick tip: Why not enhance your stay by booking a professional in-house chef, guided walk with Dartmoor's Daughter or a restorative wellbeing session with Down to Flow Escapes? Further details and recommendations are provided by Unique Homestays when booking.

From £1,995 per week | £1,495 per short break

uniquehomestays.com

Ashburton, Josh Iskander

visit
Ashburton

The ancient stannary town of Ashburton lies on the southernly edge of Dartmoor National Park. Surrounded by glorious scenery and home to an exciting array of independent shops and eateries, it's certainly worth a detour...

Start your visit at **Ashburton Craftmongers**. This truly magical shop was founded by Wildlife Cameraman Toby Strong and is managed and run by local artist Jodi Lou Parkin. Craftmongers is filled from floor to ceiling with a myriad of artisan goods and everyday treasures. Amongst its shelves you'll find hand-woven baskets, ceramics, organic beard oils and wildflower seeds. Everything is lovingly made and assigned to the artist who crafted it. The cherry on top? A portion of profits go toward supporting a Madagascan school that they built in 2020 called the 'Devon Friendship School '.

Ashburton is a mecca for interior designers and antique aficionados. No less than 12 antique and restoration shops line its quaint, winding streets, offering everything from upcycled furniture to retro reclamation. **Catherine Waters Antiques** have an eye for absurdly beautiful furniture and objet d'art, so you're bound to come away with something seriously chic. Their doors are open Thursday-Saturday, but you can also book appointments at other times.

Luxury soap makers **Odds & Suds** have a beautiful brick and mortar shop on North Street. Step inside to browse heavenly scented soaps and bath bombs, along with quality furniture and unique flea market finds. The space is tightly packed with pretty wares, so it can sometimes be a bit of a squeeze – but don't let this put you off coming away with something special!

Ashburton Delicatessen is a treasure trove of independent produce and artisan foods. This modestly sized, family-run deli attracts a stream of loyal customers, who return time and time again thanks to the sights and smells that waft from the kitchen. Likewise, **The Fish Deli** offers an array of fresh seafood and local delicacies, including lobster, River Teign mussels and plump, diver-caught scallops. There's also a well-stocked freezer of handmade ready meals.

For evening reservations, try **The Old Library Restaurant.** Run by talented local chefs, Joe Suttie and Amy Mitchell, you'll be treated to a simple yet sophisticated menu showcasing the crème de la crème of local produce. As the name suggests, the restaurant is housed inside a converted library and has bags of homegrown charm to show for it. So, pull up a chair and enjoy dishes such as fresh crab tortellini or twice-baked beetroot and cheese soufflé.

A new addition to the Ashburton restaurant scene is **Emilia.** It's the latest gourmet offering from Claire Lattin and Tom Hill, who are the restaurateurs responsible for Soho's immensely popular DUCKSOUP. Emilia is an informal Italian-style eatery on East Street where they'll be serving up dishes 'inspired by memories of their favourite Italian suppers'. So, pull up a chair at the eatery's singular large table or take a bar seat and enjoy a small daily menu that's paired with some pretty special wines.

If you want to hone your own culinary skills, book yourself a lesson at **Ashburton Cookery School & Chef's Academy.** It's one of the UK's top cookery schools and offers a huge range of classes and courses, from half day pasta making sessions to weekends devoted to artisan bread-making. The school boasts three state-of-the-art kitchens, surrounded by rolling green hills and ancient hedgerows.

If you're looking to book somewhere to stay close by, you can't go wrong with **The Hayloft**. It's a boutique property that takes self-catering to the next level with its sumptuous décor and attention to detail. Housed in a beautifully renovated 17th - century hayloft, on the edge of Dartmoor National Park, The Hayloft looks like it's been plucked straight from the pages of 'World of Interiors'.

MORE ASHBURTON

Self-Catering Properties
Ashburton Garden Flat (Airbnb)

Cafés & Bistros
The Studio Teashop
Café Latino
Rafikis

Restaurants & Bars
Arthur's at Taylors
COLJAN Bar and Restaurant
The Old Exeter Inn

Food & Drink Shops
Ella Artisan Baker
Creamo's Craft Ice Cream

Clothing Boutiques
Quirky Bird Vintage & Retro Fashion
Shakti Ellenwood Precious Jewellery
My Fabulous Things

Antique Shops
Alchemy Antiques
The Shambles
East Street Antiques
Antiques and Curios

Galleries
The Ashburn Gallery

Homewares & Gifts
POP Lights
Number 30

MAKE Southwest

bovey Tracey

MAKE Southwest is an acclaimed exhibition space for contemporary craft and design, as well as a leading charity for craft education. Located in the town of Bovey Tracey – on the edge of Dartmoor – the gallery space and shop host a rotating programme of inspiring exhibitions and events. The Guild itself contains over 250 working craftspeople, whose work is regularly showcased onsite.

The MAKE Southwest shop is the perfect place to pick up a one-of-a-kind item of jewellery, a handmade card or a unique piece of art. They exclusively stock the work of its members, and therefore there's always something original to discover.

crafts.org.uk

Saddle Tor, Paul Nash

explore

Dartmoor

Curated by Rachæl Brown

The earth feels different underfoot in Dartmoor, its granite strewn landscape only interrupted by sheep and grey houses emitting wafts of burning firewood. This harsh wilderness has different stone, woods and animals. It's these qualities that have long inspired poets and authors, and before that the folklore that seeps into the landscape. Dartmoor also means exploring. From searching for the silhouettes of the Tors, to stone circles, to the elusive Ted Hughes Memorial stone. With a new trainline opening up the area to non-drivers, Dartmoor is now ready for exploration...

Retreat to Southcombe Barn

In the heart of Dartmoor's rugged heathland Southcombe Barn has crafted a luxurious yet wild space to relax. Famous for their 'Midsummer Meadow Bed', a dramatic four-poster built out of a fallen tree, Southcombe offers a sensory night's sleep amongst the woodland of Widecombe-in-the-Moor. More impressive is their yoga studio in a converted barn and on-site art gallery that nurtures talent, carving out a space for creativity in the countryside.

Partake in local traditions

'Letterboxing' is a seriously nostalgic-feeling pastime that involves searching the windswept moors and tors for 'Letterboxes' and gathering their uniquely designed stamps along the way. Concealed in crevices and under rocks, the prospect of finding these boxes will no doubt excite scrapbookers. Sometimes they'll print an inky picture of the location, but you never know what you might find. The legendary Cranmere Pool is a good place to start, as it's home to the first letterbox. However, it does lie in Okehampton firing range, so if the red flags are up don't enter!

Marvel at a rare temperate rainforest

It's not common knowledge, but the UK is home to some of the most endangered rainforests in the world. You can find fragments of unique temperate rainforest, or 'Celtic rainforest', in different corners of the UK, but Dartmoor is home to three of the most well-known ones. You can almost smell the damp in 'Black Tor Beare' or 'Black-a-Tor Copse', an ancient oak rainforest by Okehampton where gnarled and crooked oaks are blanketed with moss and hanging lichen. Mindfully explore this druidical nature reserve by starting at the bottom of Meldon Reservoir.

Go wild swimming in south Dartmoor

Swimming in the River Dart is different to taking a dip elsewhere, thanks to the river's reddish hue and massive granite slabs. One of the most well-loved areas for freshwater bathing is Sharrah Pool. Park at Newbridge, cross the bridge then follow the woodland path to your right along the river. Tavy Cleave in west Dartmoor is another stunning spot on the River Tavy, bordered by cascades in a rugged valley. There's a couple of glassy pools along the river, so park at Lane End car park to explore them.

Live the good life in Bovey Tracey

The charming town of Bovey Tracey is home to a vareity of specialist shops. The Cheese Shed is brimming with heavy wheels of aged cheddar, oozy brie and crumbly West Country goat's cheeses. There's also Dartmoor Whisky Distillery for those who enjoy a talk about the distilling process and a taste of the bourbon cask. MAKE Southwest is a contemporary crafts gallery set in a historic riverside mill. Outside flows the River Bovey and inside exhibitions span art and traditional crafts (read more on p.70)

Meet Dartmoor's wild ponies

Few sights are quite as iconic as a herd of Dartmoor ponies grazing on the moors. If you pull into one of Dartmoor's many scenic stop off points it's highly likely you'll come face-to-face with one of these beautiful wild creatures. We don't recommend trying to interact with them, but they are rather unperturbed by human contact (they may even attempt to nibble your car wing-mirror). So, take the opportunity to snap an unforgettable photo or head to the Dartmoor Pony Heritage Trust in Bovey Tracey to learn more about them.

Immerse yourself in wildlife

The ancient woodland around Drewsteignton offers some of Dartmoor's most picturesque scenery, ripe for exploration. Start at Fingle Bridge, the gateway to Fingle Woods and the River Teign, where there are Victorian plunge pools and wild swimming spots. The unspoilt Teign Gorge hums with wildlife: otters, salmon and kingfishers can all be found here and you might see the flash of a roe or fallow deer. For guaranteed views, head to Castle Drogo, a 20th -century estate managed by the National Trust.

Get swept away in folklore at Belstone Tor

On the edge of wild north Dartmoor, by the River Taw, Belstone Tor crowns the top of a string of tors. Ramble up this granite peak for breathtaking panoramic views; in clear weather you can even spy the North Devon coast. It's worth stopping off at The Nine Maidens stone circle en route, a site immersed in folklore, supposedly being nine women who were condemned to stone after dancing on the Sabbath.

Feast on a rustic pub lunch

Eversfield Organic's delightful Dartmoor Inn is a whitewashed pub nestled in west Dartmoor's Merrivale. With sweeping views of the dramatic moors, it's the perfect place to feast and sink a traditional ale after a hike. Surrounding the pub are clusters of stone circles, prehistoric ritual sites and standing stones from Bronze Age settlements. As part of the Eversfield Organic group, you can imagine the quality of the food on offer. Look forward to seasonal menus, locally sourced produce and a zero-waste ideology.

Go stargazing on a clear night

The wide open skies above Dartmoor are perfect for a spot of stargazing. For dazzling nocturnal sights try Piddledown Common at Castle Drogo. Not only can you catch the stars here but the area comes alive with wildlife at night (listen out for Tawny owls and bats). You could also park your car in remote Haytor Car Park and walk up to Haytor rocks. From here you can gaze up at the stars free from nearby light pollution.

MORE DARTMOOR

Self-Catering Properties
Moorland View Cottage, North Bovey
The Riddle, North Bovey

Hotels
The Horn of Plenty, Tavistock
Bovey Castle, Bovey
Gidleigh Park, Chagford
Hotel Endsleigh, Milton Abbot

Cafés & Restaurants
Café on the Green, Widecombe
The Birdcage, Chagford
The Cornish Arms, Tavistock

Food & Drink Shops
Dartmoor Deli, Tavistock
Eversfield Organic Farmshop, Tavistock
Jaded Palates Wines, Chagford

Homewares & Lifestyle
ARTISAN The Makers' Shop, Chagford
Rue des Fontenelles, Chagford

Lemons Cottage

atherington

In the picture postcard village of Atherington sits Lemons Cottage: a 16th-century property with a thoroughly modern attitude. Pushing open the solid oak door reveals a cosy home-from-home with rustic stone floors, original beams and an exposed brick fireplace. But this Tudor cottage offers so much more than pretty period features. Guests have access to all the mod cons they could desire, from superfast fibre broadband to underfloor heating. Head to the cinema room to take advantage of the 75" television complete with surround sound, Netflix and Playstation 4. Or pour yourself a glass of wine and soak away your stresses in the baby pink freestanding bathtub. Set in its own country gardens, Lemons Cottage is the ideal bolthole from which to explore everything North Devon has to offer. You'll find a myriad of beaches just a short drive away, including surfing paradise Croyde Bay.

Maverick tip: On a sunny morning the garden is the perfect spot for an al fresco brunch accompanied by birdsong and the gentle babble of the nearby stream.

From £235 per night,
book via: sandandstoneescapes.com

Ilfracombe, Collette Dyson

explore

North Devon

Curated by Lucy Shrimpton

While South Devon rolls out her riviera, North is her more secretive sister, an altogether wilder character of cliffs, caves and coves, gifting not only a restorative sense of remoteness but a whole host of refreshingly authentic experiences that continue to uplift long after you've left. From the scoop of Bideford Bay, up the surf-poised and sandy Saunton, Croyde and Woolacombe, and around the bend into the enchanting playground of woods, streams and velvety moss that is Exmoor – North Devon's landscapes and lifestyle template reward the slow explorer.

BIDEFORD BAY

Old trumping new is North Devon's recurring vibe and you'll get it stepping over the threshold of Bideford's **Old Bridge Antiques**, four floors of curios getting a second innings at life. There's another time-travelling element at the region's '**Pannier Markets**' — not a fleeting retail trend but a regular means of shopping in Devon for nigh on 150 years. While Bideford's and Barnstaple's have converted their old Butchers' Rows into artisan studios and independent trader units, their foodie halls share an atmosphere with grand and bustling Victorian train stations. In between, there's the pretty waterside village of Appledore. Check out the pastel-hued fishermen's cottages and make a beeline for **Appledore Crafts Company** where our hankering is for Lucy Turner's willow basketry.

EAT AT: The Glorious Oyster in Instow, a tucked-away seafood shack, oyster bar and beach café with occasional tunes in the dunes. Alternatively, head to Woolfardisworthy (pronounced 'Woolsery') to dine at popular gastro pub, The Farmers Arms (pictured right)

STAY AT: Loveland Farm about 20 minutes west of Bideford. It's an eco-retreat with easy-on-the-eye dome pods giving the place all the feels of a fresh-air hotel. South of Barnstaple, Vintage Vardos delivers gypsy glamping alongside a bubbling stream.

THERE'S DEVON TREASURE AT:
Bideford's Burton Art Gallery, a dynamic cultural space showcasing the works of makers such as Helyne Jennings.

BRAUNTON TO MORTEHOE

Don't resist the urge to break into Kate Bush's 'The Sensual World' as you enter Braunton Burrows – the labyrinthine vastness, cascading sand, and wildflower spectrum of the UK's largest natural dune system will all compel you to do so. There's similar headiness on tap at surfy Croyde, courtesy of waves battering you to a welcome state of invigoration before you retreat to the thatchy-yet-not-twee village. In the Famous-Five-vibes village of Mortehoe, an old-world micro-museum is jam-packed with maritime echoes such as vintage cameras, sea-smooth bottles, and monochrome photos – all shining a light on a coast of wreckers and smugglers.

EAT AT: Barricane Beach at Woolacombe – a cove of exotic shells, rock pools and a beach hut for a curry and sunset combo.

STAY AT: Swell Yoga offering Devon-heaven retreats combining surf lessons, Vinyasa yoga, glamping and fresh meals served by a vegan chef.

THERE'S DEVON TREASURE AT:
Saunton Sands Hotel's Source Spa thanks to a marine thermal suite, sun deck, dune view pool and ice fountain.

ILFRAMCOMBE TO COMBE MARTIN

Ilfracombe, metropolitan by contrast, is famous for its curious and cool Victorian seabathing 'Tunnels' complex, as well as Verity – Damien Hirst's divisive quayside sculpture (we're with Damien, for the record). If your retail maxim is that it's better to mine a small number of boutiques properly rather than gloss over too many, all roads lead to an increasingly artisanal smattering in Fore Street, including Juul-at-Home for gifts and lifestyle, and FortyThree, a co-op of locally inspired art, textiles, ceramics, glass, and paper. Heading east, the craggy coast throws up some great secluded swim spots: nudie ones at the evocatively named Wild Pear Beach or less cheeky ones at Broadsands.

EAT AT: Michelin-starred Thomas Carr 1873, or Stacc if you're just after cocktails and patisserie to (dare we say it) put the Devonshire cream tea in the shade.

STAY AT: The Earlsdale B&B in Ilfracombe or The Old Apple Store in Lee (part of the Boutique Retreats collection).

THERE'S DEVON TREASURE AT:
Hand:Plant in Ilfracombe – a gallery, café, workshop space and plantery – all under one roof and all with a sustainable focus. We love Justine Hartley's locally made blankets: Devon hygge, if you like.

ON TO EXMOOR...

With dramatic sights like the South West Coast
Path's Valley of Rocks and Lynton's extraordinary
cliff railway, it's perhaps not all that surprising that
the coast steals the limelight from the moorland.
But poking around just a little inland is so worth
the detour. Exmoor National Park, for starters, was
Europe's first Dark Sky Reserve, and on Barton
Farm's stargazing soirées it's something as
accessible to night sky newbies as it is to niche
enthusiasts. Come equipped with binoculars and
a hungry tum (the evening also involves pizza
making) and keep your fingers crossed for the
Rings of Saturn, Jupiter's stripes and the Orion
Nebula. For anyone with literary leanings, there's
Wild About Exmoor's guided walks in Lorna
Doone country, taking in the church where
(spoiler alert) the author imagined the infamous
altar shooting.

EAT AT: The gorgeous Coach House at
Kentisbury Grange Hotel. The French might call
this eatery 'bistronomique', meaning gastro food
with a laid-back ambiance.

STAY AT: Rockton Mews in Lynton, part of the
Boutique Retreats collection. It's the last house
before the dramatically beautiful Valley of Rocks.

THERE'S DEVON TREASURE AT:

Indicknowle Farm where you can buy cider at
source, the methods unchanged and in the same
family since the 1870s. You might have to holler
for someone; it's not so much a shop as a
working farm.

MORE NORTH DEVON

Hotels:
Saunton Sands Hotel
Woolacombe Bay Hotel

Self-Catering:
Braunds Sail Loft (Airbnb)
Rockton Mews
Lower Birch Farmhouse

Camping & Glamping:
Stargazer Pod, Loveland Farm
The Ark at Leewood

Restaurants & Bistros:
The Lost Kitchen, Tiverton
Pynes Arms, nr Barnstaple
The Glorious Oyster, Instow
Pattard Restaurant, Hartland

Food & Drink Shops:
Johns of Instow & Appledore

24 hours in

Clovelly

A trip to North Devon wouldn't be complete without visiting Clovelly. Often hailed as 'the gem in North Devon's crown', this chocolate-box village hugs the steep cliffside and meanders down to a beautiful historic harbour. Idyllic white-washed cottages, cobbled lanes and colourful fishing boats make this village very photogenic indeed. What's more, there are no cars allowed, so sledges are enlisted to help locals get from A to B...

Mention Clovelly to most people and the first thing that comes to mind is donkeys. These adorable creatures pulled coaches and carriages up and down the village lanes in the days before motor cars, but today Clovelly donkeys enjoy a much more restful existence. You're likely to find them grazing in the meadow at the top of the village and they're all too happy to pose for photographs.

Clovelly Court Gardens offer quite the contrast to the rustic vibes of the town. Rows of neat, carefully tended gardens are sheltered within its walls and visitors are invited to stroll around its colourful flower beds for a small admission fee.

The Clovelly arts and crafts scene is surprisingly vibrant. We're particularly fond of the work of Lydia Jane Duncan, who runs a gallery and studio in the town called **Candyland Studios**. Also new to the scene is **Original Artifacts.** The brainchild of local resident Rebecca Taylor, it stocks an eclectic mix of both found and foraged treasures alongside artisan crafts made by people living in the village and surrounding area.

Chief among the town's eateries is **The Harbour Restaurant** at **The Red Lion Inn**. Fresh fish, vegetables and game are delivered from the nearby estate or landed daily right on its doorstep. Feast on famous Clovelly lobsters (when they're in season) and take in the blue harbour views with a glass of wine.

There's a small admission fee of £8.25 to visit Clovelly, which contributes to maintenance and upkeep of the village.

Clovelly Harbour. Lynsey Taylor

Exeter

The historic city of Exeter is widely regarded as the cultural capital of Devon. From its extraordinary cathedral to its picturesque quayside and vibrant independent shopping scene, there's plenty to discover during your visit...

Start your trip to Exeter in the heart of the city: the Cathedral Green. Construction of Exeter Cathedral on the present site began as early as 1114 AD, so take the rare opportunity to explore one the finest examples of Gothic architecture in the world. Inside, the cathedral's impressive vaulted ceiling is a sight to behold, but to truly appreciate its magnificence you should opt for a rooftop tour, as the views over the city are spectacular.

Overlooking the Cathedral Green is **The Ivy Exeter.** As part of the iconic Ivy Collection, this laidback restaurant is the perfect setting for a relaxed yet sophisticated meal. Inside, ceilings climb high and large windows fill the space with light. Décor is a riot of colour, with beautiful floral-inspired wallpapers and banquettes adding to a sense of informal luxury.

Gandy Street (pictured left) is a vibrant cobbled street that's home to a myriad of independent shops, from artisanal chocolatiers to antique jewellers. Multi-disciplinary art venue **The Phoenix Centre** sits at the top of Gandy Street (look out for the enormous metal phoenix guarding its entrance). The centre connects filmmakers, dancers, DJs, drag performers, musicians and anyone interested in creativity through frequent workshops and exhibitions. Pop in for a pint in their bar before catching live shows or arthouse films.

Chococo's colourful signage will no doubt tempt you inside, where you can browse their tempting range of award-winning chocolates or sip on local Crankhouse coffee. It goes without saying that their artisan chocolate truffles are the main lure, but there's also Chococo gelato, brownies, cakes and bakes to enjoy.

The Exploding Bakery Cafe by Modern House

Elsewhere on Gandy Street, **Red Panda** rustles up big, Asian street food flavours. Their colourful takeout menu features everything from fluffy bao buns to spicy tofu salads, each made using fresh south west ingredients.

For sit down food, head to **The Cork and Tile.** They serve up Portuguese cuisine and tapas, so you can expect a sizeable menu of authentic, bite-sized dishes. All bases are covered, from crispy cod fritters to traditional Portuguese stews.

Whether you've got kids in tow or you're just young at heart, **The Royal Albert Memorial Museum (RAMM)** is fun for the whole family. This world-class museum tells the story of Exeter and Devon from the prehistoric era to the present, along with interactive exhibits and a beautifully curated gift shop.

Across the road from RAMM is **Hyde & Seek.** This vibrant shop is a celebration of all things bright and colourful, offering quirky and fun products at affordable prices. It's a one-stop-shop for gifting, as you can buy everything from eco-friendly presents and funky homewares to wrapping paper and cards.

If coffee and cake is on the agenda, get over to **The Exploding Bakery Café** next to Central Station. This laidback venue is a saving grace for commuters and shoppers looking for a quality flat white and a spot of people watching. We recommend getting yourself a piece of the sour cherry & pistachio polenta cake or a slice of their delicious almond brownie...

Rendezvous wine bar is one of Exeter's best kept secrets. This intimate basement venue has an exceptional wine list featuring over 60 suggestions from across the globe – as well as famous Champagnes and local spirits. There's also an ever-changing menu of west country cuisine on offer and a peaceful, secluded garden to enjoy in the summer months.

Harry's Restaurant on Longbrook Street is a real Exeter institution. Established in 1993 by the Pounds family, this relaxed but beautifully outfitted restaurant has earned itself a glowing reputation. Between gourmet burgers and flat iron steaks, laidback brunches and a cookie dough dessert that's to die for, there really is something for everyone. Just make sure you book ahead of time because Harry's is one popular joint!

Exeter's Fore Street is home to some of the best independent shops in the city. Tucked away in McCoy's Arcade is plant-based café and brunch spot Sacred Grounds. Tuck into crispy waffles and vegan wraps or order a calming beetroot latte and spend your morning in the warm, light atrium of the arcade.

Elsewhere in McCoy's you'll find The Real McCoy, purveyors of vintage clothing and accessories. They stock everything from retro varsity jackets and Levi jeans to beaded gowns from the roaring '20s. There's also independent bookshop Bookbag contained within the arcade's walls, as well as indie gems like Exeter Tea Merchants, and Hops + Crafts.

Pack your Kilner jars and head to Zero Exeter for eco essentials and planet-friendly homewares. Their reclaimed shelves are filled with a wide array of package free goods, from dried spices to refillable oils and cleaning products. There's also plenty of locally made, artisanal products on sale, as well as stylish reusable bottles and coffee cups.

Exeter Quayside is our favourite part of the city, thanks to its eclectic mix of cafés, restaurants and shops overlooking the water. We suggest hiring a canoe or a kayak and heading downstream to Double Locks – an 18th -century inn with plenty of outdoor seating and warming log fires inside. Alternatively, keep your feet on dry land and stroll along the quayside before heading to On The Waterfront for one of their famous 16-inch dustbin lid pizzas.

Elsewhere on the quay is Topham Brewery – a microbrewery and tap house that's one of the hottest spots for music in town. On summer nights, you can take a seat on the historic quayside and listen to live performances under the twinkling lights, with a craft beer in hand.

Red Brick Barn by Matthew Heritage

Exe Valley Glamping by Matthew Heritage

MORE EXETER

Hotels
Southernhay House
Townhouse Exeter

Self-Catering
Kings of the Swingers (Plum Guide)
The Redbrick Barn
The Old Piggery, Windout Farm

Camping & Glamping
Exe Valley Glamping

Cafés & Bistros
Pink Moon Café & Club
Veg Box Café
Artigianos
Grow Coffee House
March Coffee
Exe Coffee Roasters

Restaurants & Bars
Stage
The Conservatory
Sabatini
Doctor Ink's Curiosities

Food & Drink Shops
Magdalen Cheese & Provisions
Farm to Folk
Pullo

Clothing Boutiques
Lorna Ruby
Crede Boutique

Homewares & Lifestyle
Moko
Maker Mart
Hutch Houseplants
Along avec Anna
Leaf Street Exeter
Soap Daze
Bracket (Interiors)

Experiences
The One Mile Bakery
Quayside Distillery & Bar
Northcote Theatre
Exeter Corn Exchange

Dukes

sidmouth

Ask any Sidmouth local where to eat and we guarantee
they'll point you in the direction of Dukes. This thoroughly
modern seaside inn is a true Sidmouth mainstay, just 30
steps from the beach and slap bang in the centre of the
esplanade. It serves some of the best beer battered fish &
chips around, along with an impressive range of drinks and
cocktails. Dukes' all-day dining has something for everyone,
with plenty of pub classics, fresh seafood, local meats, and
plant-based options on the menu. So, order one of their
popular crab sarnies and head for the outside patio area. It's
the perfect spot to breathe in the sea air and enjoy lunch
with friends. If an evening reservation is on the cards, then
there's 14 comfy bedrooms upstairs, so you can make the
most of their cocktail list.

Maverick Tip: If you've got a sweet tooth you need to try
Dukes speciality hot chocolate. It's an impressive mug of
cocoa with a tower of whipped cream, mini marshmallows,
and a chocolate flake for good measure.

dukessidmouth.co.uk

Beer Village

discover

East Devon

East Devon is a patchwork of green fields,
busy market towns and quaint coastal
communities. It boasts more than its fair share
of award-winning restaurants and it's home to
some of our favourite independent shops
and businesses...

There's something magical about the coastal village of **Beer**. The high street and surrounding lanes look like they've been plucked straight from a bygone era, and its shingle beach is flanked by steep chalk cliffs and studded with colourful deckchairs and fishing boats. It's the perfect spot for a cool dip in the sea or you can pull up a chair at Ducky's and tuck into a fresh crab sandwich made right by the water.

Close by is the market town of Axminster – home to **Collate Interiors** and its bijou tearoom **The Tiffin Box**. From the vintage crockery down to the original black and white chequered floor, both businesses blend the traditional with a touch of eccentricity. Collate brings together quality pieces by small-scale southwest makers, while The Tiffin Box serves up tasty homemade cake by the slice.

Head to **Trinity Hill Nature Reserve** to stretch your legs and soak in the woodland scenery. This natural oasis is located close to Axminster town and boasts a network of footpaths and striking views over the Axe Valley. You can spy unique varieties of moth nestling in the heather here and you may even catch sight of a lizard during the summer months.

Nearby **River Cottage HQ** was made famous by Hugh Fearnley-Whittingstall's television series of the same name. It's a working farm and cookery school that teaches back-to-basics courses where you can learn essential skills such as bread making, foraging and fish filleting. Similarly, anyone who's keen to learn how to cook with fire ought to book a session at **High Grange Cookery School**. At this rural retreat you can learn all the essentials of British outdoor cooking.

Glebe House is a guest house, restaurant and 15-acre smallholding in Southleigh, Colyton. This charming venue boasts far-reaching views over the rolling hills of the Coly Valley, and is only a short drive from the Jurassic Coast. Décor takes its cue from the lush, country surroundings, with five guest bedrooms and an annexe designed with bold use of colour and patterns, and artistic details and murals throughout.

If small batch ice-cream and crispy stone-baked pizzas sound good to you, you'll probably love **Otter Valley Field Kitchen**. Housed in a contemporary, glass-sided barn, this café is located moments from the A30, making it perfect for breaking up long car journeys. All of their ice-creams are made using milk from their own dairy herd, who you often see grazing the fields as you tuck into your lunch.

The market town of Honiton was once internationally famed for its lace and pottery industries. Today, it's widely regarded as the antiques capital of Devon and still boasts a hugely independent High Street. When the sun is shining there's no better place to enjoy a cup of tea and a slice of cake than in **Toast Café & Patisserie**'s enchanting garden. Shaded by vines and home to songbirds and apple trees, this al fresco spot is seriously charming.

Family-run pub **The Holt** sits across the road from Toast. Upstairs, you'll find its popular restaurant, where menus shift with the seasons and pub favourites can be enjoyed year-round. Meanwhile downstairs is a lively pub that pours pints of their own range of Otter Brewery beers.

Look out for the newest addition to Honiton High Street: **GENESIS**. This exciting venture is putting your five-a-day back on the menu and giving a 21st-century twist to the traditional greengrocers. Expect the shelves to be packed with the freshest, locally-grown fruit and veg, along with some addictively good sourdough bread.

On the outskirts of Honiton is **Combe Garden Centre.** This trendy garden nursery sells a huge selection of plants, but we mostly visit for their fabulous café, 'The Kitchen'. Its beautifully landscaped garden is one of our favourite places to grab a bite to eat with friends.

Find **The Pig - at Combe** (pictured right) in the picture-perfect village of Gittisham. This gorgeous Elizabethan country house hotel boasts 30 bespoke rooms, lush country gardens, a restaurant and sweeping valley views. The Pig turns the traditional layout of a country house on its head, so walking through its 16th-century doors takes you straight into its wood-panelled bar. Here, you can take a seat by the fireplace and sip on botanical cocktails inspired by the onsite herb gardens.

The Pig Hotel, Jake Eastham

The seaside town of Sidmouth was apparently Jane Austen's staycation destination of choice, and unsurprisingly the town has retained much of its regency charm. There are no flashy restaurants or retro amusements to be found on the esplanade, but you can stroll along the quaint seafront and grab a cone of fish and chips to eat by the sea. The town is part of the world- famous Jurassic Coast which is a UNESCO World Heritage Site. Its iconic red cliffs are thousands of years old and bookend the town's shingle beaches, which are great for sea swimming.

A short drive from Sidmouth is **The Donkey Sanctuary**. For over 50 years this hugely successful charity has worked tirelessly to transform the lives of donkeys across the globe. A visit to the sanctuary lets you experience their work firsthand and gives you the opportunity to get up close to the rescue donkeys, who are seriously cute. It's a great day out if you've got little ones in tow and there's also a bright and airy café onsite that serves coffees with donkey latte art (just incase you needed another reasons to visit!).

The charming coastal town of Budleigh Salterton boasts a long, pebbly seafront with colourful beach huts and a largely indepedent high street. We usually grab an ice cream cone and stroll along the seafront, picturing ourselves living in one of the many gorgeous Dutch-style homes. But if it's coffee you're after head to **Brook Kitchen Art Café**. It's a friendly spot that serves breakfast, lunch and coffee, as well as tapas on Friday evenings. The café is adjoined to **Brook Gallery**, who specialise in original prints and represent some of the most influential artists in the UK today.

The town of **Exmouth** draws in a much younger crowd. Its two miles of golden sands make it ideal for swimming and it's filled with family-friendly amusements and places to eat. If you love houseplants as much as we do then visit **The House of Plants** (above) on Exmouth High Street. They stock everything from teeny tiny cacti to towering Bird of Paradise. Plus, they offer plant workshops and a bespoke plant styling service.

Exmouth's Sideshore Development has plenty to offer, from water sports to beachside restaurants. **Café Patisserie Glacerie** was established by local celebrity chef, Michael Caines and his Head Pastry Chef, Sylvain Peltier. It's a trendy venue with pastel coloured walls and some extremely Instagram-worthy pastries. At peak times, queues can get long, but the gelato is worth the wait. There's also **EDGE Watersports.** Headed up by world champion kite surfer Steph Bridge, they offer lessons and kit hire for everything from power kiting to SUP and beach yoga.

Lympstone Manor (pictured left) is a historic Grade II-listed Georgian manor house that has been transformed into a contemporary hotel for the 21st century. Chef patron Michael Caines is the man behind the manor, drawing on a wealth of experience to create an idyllic retreat by the picturesque Exe Estuary. Each of the hotel's luxurious suites feature sumptuous décor and complimentary gin trays. What's more, rooms are named after different birds native to the nearby estuary – a charming touch that weaves the hotel's interiors into the surrounding landscape.

MORE EAST DEVON

Self-Catering
River Cottage, Axminster

The Beach House, Exmouth

Camping & Glamping
Cuckoo Down Farm, West Hill

Lower Keats Glamping, Axminster

Cafés & Bistros
The Grazing Cow, Offwell

Heron Farm, Honiton

JK's Bistro, Honiton

Shopping
Greendale Farm Shop, nr Exeter

The Tipsy Merchant, Budleigh Salterton

Otterton Mill, Budleigh Salterton

Apothespa, Sidmouth

Coldharbour Farm Shop, Ottery St Mary

Galleries
Hybrid Gallery, Honiton

Self-Cater Sidmouth

sidmouth

Staycationing in Sidmouth has never been easier – or more stylish – thanks to the town's most talked about self-catering properties. Self-Cater Sidmouth offers its guests three beautifully outfitted properties in unrivalled locations, each within easy reach of the beach or just a short stroll to the town centre.

'The Townhouse' is perfect for group holidays, boasting four spacious rooms, a communal kitchen, a chilled TV room and a private courtyard garden, complete with BBQ and bar. Meanwhile, 'The Apartment' is a three-bed, loft-style living space in the centre of town. The state-of-the-art kitchen leads into a stylish dining and lounge space that's perfect for socialising with friends.

We love 'Cobbers Cottage' most of all – it's a 13th-century fisherman's cottage with bags of character and modern scandi beach styling. It's only 25 metres from the seafront, so you can rise with the sun and take a dip in the sea or recharge after a day spent exploring the coast path.

Maverick tip: Don't fancy cooking? Head over to Dukes on the seafront for plate of fish & chips.

selfcatersidmouth.co.uk

24 hours in
Topsham

Picturesque Topsham is nestled on the east bank of the Exe Estuary, just a stone's throw from the cathedral city of Exeter. It's a charming waterside town with plenty of independent shops and restaurants to discover. Start your visit at the bustling quayside, where you can sink a pint with locals at **The Lighter Inn** or mill around **Quay Antiques Centre**. The latter is a three-story warehouse packed to the rafters with over 60 dealers showcasing collectables and curiosities. There's always a bargain to be had amongst its shelves, as they glitter with antique jewellery, silver tableware and vintage paraphernalia.

Swot up on local history at **Topsham Museum**. The museum itself is rather photogenic, as it's housed in a 17th -century, Dutch-style building that overlooks the estuary. It once served as the home of a wealthy Exeter merchant, but today it showcases a collection of intriguing artefacts, each highlighting an aspect of Topsham's colourful maritime history.

Topsham's foodie credentials are top notch and for a small town it's awash with places to eat or grab a coffee. You won't miss **Sara's Petite Cuisine** thanks to its blushed pink façade and cascading roses (à la Peggy Porschen). This bijou patisserie is a big hit with locals. Owner Sara Felix was raised in Devon but originally hails from Portugal, which explains why her pastéis de nata are to die for. It's hard to choose between her delicate fruit tarts or her colourful cupcakes, so do yourself a favour and just try both!

For the best coffee in town get over to **Circle** at 37 Fore Street. Owners David and Faye Clement know their piccolo from their macchiato and can pour an outstanding flat white. They're also big supporters of the Devon arts scene, so you'll find work by local artists and craftspeople for sale in the shop, along with a fabulous selection of houseplants.

There's something rather special about **The Salutation Inn.** Though it's set within one of Topsham's oldest buildings (a 1720s coaching inn) this hotel and restaurant is a thoroughly modern affair. We suggest booking afternoon tea in the sunny courtyard or experiencing their popular tasting menu in the dazzling GlassHouse Restaurant (where fine dining dishes can be enjoyed under the starry night sky).

If dirty burgers and smoky ribs are more your bag, you ought to try **The Pig & Pallet**. They're specialists in all things carnivorous, so meaty platters and craft beers are the name of the game. The team cure, butcher, and barbecue their meats in a traditional and ethical way, which is abundantly clear in the quality of their scran. The smokehouse is open Wednesday - Sunday, so park your car at Topsham Quay and follow your nose to find your way there (you'll know what we mean when you get your first whiff of that smoky aroma).

The Boathouse Café is tucked away on a quiet street just off the quay. It's a real continental affair, offering a stripped-back menu of tasty crêpes, galettes and baguettes. They're also fully licensed and host regular cocktail evenings on Thursdays and Fridays.

We could easily spend an afternoon browsing Topsham's many galleries and boutiques and our first port of call is usually **Nest Living** (right). As the name suggests, this charming shop offers a curated collection of gifts and accessories to make your nest a relaxing and joyous space. On its shelves you'll find everything from handmade chocolates to essential oil body wash, soft alpaca wool socks, and calming pillow mist. They also stock preloved clothes, pretty stationery and uplifting homeware to embellish your own nest with.

For ladies' clothes, try **Siena Boutique.** Here, you can browse rails of beautifully made Scandinavian clothing and jewellery. There's also **Allotment**, where you can find plenty of luxurious wardrobe essentials and a myriad of fashion and lifestyle brands, from Nailberry to Maison Hotel.

For art aficionados, **Artenax** sells a range of contemporary art and homewares that will bring a splash of colour to your home. There's also the stylish **Flemming & Sell** where you can browse work by artist Charlottle Flemming along with homewares from brands such as Abigail Ahern.

a charming waterside town, with plenty of independent shops and eateries

To make the most of the local scenery you can rent a bike from **Route 2 Bikes** near the quay and cycle along the scenic Exe Estuary Trail. Alternatively, pack your swimming costume and take a plunge in Topsham's outdoor swimming pool. It's heated to a pleasant 28 degrees and open April to September.

A short walk from Topsham will take you to **Darts Farm.** Well-heeled locals flock to this nationally award-winning farm shop for its artisanal food hall and fabulous onsite restaurants. Stock up on artisan breads, local wines, craft beers, handmade chutneys and much more. It's not just about the food though. For home and lifestyle inspiration, they have the iconic specialist retailers, such as Fired Earth, AGA and Orange Tree. Don't miss Cow & Cacao Café for indulgent homemade waffles and artisan gelato sundaes.

MORE TOPSHAM

Cafés & Bistros
The Jar Bakery
The Café

Restaurants & Bars
The Galley Restaurant
Marcello
Denley's Essence of India

Homewares & Lifestyle
Lark
Squid & The Kid
CASA
Amos Lighting + Home
Ebb & Flow Home
Mere Antiques
Country Cheeses
Cooks Aweigh

Maverick loves

Unique hideaways

Unique hideaways is a bespoke collection of one-of-a-kind places to stay in hidden corners across the UK. From clifftop cabins with unbeatable sea views to quirky glamping abodes tucked away in the forest, each of their hideaways is truly out of the ordinary. Their portfolio of hidden havens promises to take you on a journey into nature, giving you the opportunity to re-wild yourself all while staying in a little bit of luxury. From the sandy shores of Cornwall to the remote charm of Pembrokeshire, explore wild coastline, gorgeous countryside, and the ever-beautiful areas across the UK.

We love their collection of Devon hideaways. Choose from a myriad of properties, from a romantic Mongolian yurt in the North Devon countryside to a beautifully repurposed Californian Airsteam near Exeter. Get ready to take the plunge with a spot of wild swimming, watch the twinkle of the night sky from your very own hot tub, cosy up in front of a wood-burner, or toast marshmallows and tell stories over a crackling firepit. Your dream getaway should be for making memories, so turn the page to discover three of our favourite Unique hideaways in Devon...

Whittlers Yurt

nr clovelly

Whittlers Yurt is a romantic bolthole for two, nestled in the tranquil North Devon countryside. This authentic Mongolian round yurt is perfect for embracing a slower pace of life. It's sumptuously decked out with eclectic furniture and features a playful blend of patterns, colours and luxurious soft furnishings. On a rainy day you can light the wood-burner and cosy up on the ornate rattan armchair with your favourite book in hand. Rest your head on the sumptuous, pink velvet bed and wake up with the sunrise, as light pours in through the window.

Outside, the yurt benefits from a private deck, complete with a covered sunshade area and a private hot tub. There's also a small but perfectly equipped kitchen to be found in its own handcrafted wooden shed. The kitchen contains everything you could need to whip up a tasty meal for two, or you can fire up the barbecue for a spot of al fresco dining in the sunshine.

Maverick Tip: Whittlers Yurt has access to the owners' lake. Follow the babbling stream to find a perfectly placed platform for meditation or yoga. Alternatively, if you're feeling brave you can cool off with a spot of wild swimming.

From £110 per night,
Book via uniquehideaways.com

California Dreaming

nr exeter

This next hideaway is quite the hidden gem. It's a refurbished Californian Airstream that glistens in the Devonshire sunshine and provides the perfect base from which to explore the local countryside. Step through its pristine aluminium doors to be greeted by airy and surprisingly spacious interiors. California Dreaming benefits from plenty of natural light and boasts a well-equipped kitchen, a beautifully finished bathroom and an open-plan living space. Despite its retro, Americana aesthetic, this stylish hideaway comes equipped with many of the creature comforts you'd expect to find at home. Integrated roof fans and modern central heating make sure that, whatever the season, the temperature is just right, while a SMART TV sits above the folding dining area. Tucked into the rear of the Airstream sits a luxurious king-size bed which, with its plush bedding and cosy placement, ensures a great night's sleep after a day of adventures. Wake to the sound of gentle birdsong echoing across the neighbouring meadow and start your day with a hearty American-style breakfast.

Maverick Tip: The Airstream has its own Ooni pizza oven, so you can take turns tossing your own pizzas and crisping them to perfection. Alternatively, book dinner at The Ley Arms — a 13th-century thatched pub that's only a five-minute walk away.

From £130 per night,
Book via uniquehideaways.com

Rosie's Hut

nr Totnes

This spectacular shepherd's hut is set among acres of stunning grounds and surrounded by lush Devonshire farmland. Stroll along your very own nature trail through woodland and wildflower meadows or simply sit on your own private patio and soak in the views. Inside Rosie's Hut is a romantic yet quirky space, with traditional planked walls and calming green paintwork throughout. At one end of the hut you'll find a king-sized bed and a window that boasts views of field and sky as far as the eye can see. In the centre of the hut, there's a beautiful, bijou kitchen with a full-sized ceramic butler's sink, double hob, and plenty of worktop space. And at the other end you can enjoy an en suite shower room. After dark, strings of fairy lights lend a magical atmosphere to the hut. You can count the stars in the night sky above and pour yourself a glass of bubbles as you relax and unwind in the wood-fired hot tub.

Maverick Tip: Rosie's Hut is perfectly located for exploring the South Hams. There are plenty of beaches right on your doorstep, including Blackpool Sands, where you can hire kayaks, body boards, and paddle boards.

From £50 per night,
Book via uniquehideaways.com

Maverick Loves

The Devon
Restaurant Scene

Devon is home to a myriad of outstanding eateries, from exquite fine dining venues to rustic country pubs. The county has stacked up several Michelin Stars and AA Rosettes, but its rustic fare is just as appetising. Across the next few pages we've rounded up several of our favourite foodie destinations, including country house hotels and a unique floating restaurant...

The Elephant Restaurant is the crème de la crème of Torbay's food and drink scene. It's a bright and informal restaurant that has enjoyed over 15 years of Michelin star status thanks to the hard work of chef proprietor Simon Hulstone and his wife Katy. Guests are invited to dine in a laidback, brasserie-style space that offers calming views of Torquay's blue marina. Though the setting is relaxed, the food is rather special. Expect beautifully presented dishes that will knock your socks off!

The Angel - Taste of Devon is an absolute treat for lovers of fine dining. Sat on Dartmouth's South Embankment, overlooking the picturesque River Dart, the building itself has a vibrant culinary past. It first opened its doors as The Carved Angel back in 1974 – under famed chef Joyce Molyneux – and quickly became regarded as one of the finest restaurants in the country. Today, reinvented as The Angel - Taste of Devon, Head Chef Elly Wentworth is at the restaurant's helm, cooking up a rather extraordinary menu with her talented young kitchen team.

Twenty Seven by Jamie Rogers is flying the flag for Kingsbridge cuisine. The restaurant is housed in a former warehouse in the centre of town and has gained an enviable reputation for its exquisite food and signature presentation. Expect meticulously crafted tasting menus that showcase the finest local produce and some out-of-the-box drink pairings to perfectly complement your food.

Lovers of proper pub grub need to try **The Bear & Blacksmith** in Chillington. This rustic venue is near obsessive about locally made and locally sourced produce. Not only do they maintain their own vegetable and herb plot, but they also supply customers with pork, chicken and lamb that is raised on their South Allington farm. The result of this commitment to low food miles is a menu of tried-and-tested pub classics, served in a convivial atmosphere.

Fine dining doesn't get much better than the cuisine at **Lympstone Manor**. Each of the hotel's three exquisite dining rooms is overseen by celebrity chef, Michael Caines and offers award-winning menus that showcase modern European cuisine at its finest. Expect plenty of gels, delicate portions, and avant-garde plating. If you aren't a fan of nouvelle cuisine you may want to give this one a miss, but if you are then this manor house hotel should be at the top of your gourmet bucket list.

Since 1999 **Rodean Restaurant** in Kenton has been widely regarded as one of the best places to dine in Devon. Overlooking a quaint village green, this small family-run restaurant serves fine dining dishes without the price tag or pretensions. Their menus are a celebration of Devon's coast and countryside, with only the freshest ingredients gracing plates. Watch out for their monthly wine and dine events, as well as their popular their Sunday lunches.

Exmouth is home to Devon's most unique eatery: **The River Exe Café**. The only way to reach this popular venue is by water taxi because it's located offshore in the middle of the Exe Estuary. Yes, you read that correctly – it's Devon's only floating restaurant. We're still not entirely sure how to describe the sensation of sipping cocktails and tucking into your lunch on a gently bobbing pontoon; but the delicious menus and 360 views make The River Exe Café worth experiencing!

Don't let **The Masons Arms'** chocolate box façade fool you. This 13th-century thatched pub might seem perfectly unsassuming from the outside but housed within its walls is an exceptional fine dining experience. It's safe to say that chef patron Mark Dobson has mastered the art of classic French cuisine. Having earned his spurs at The Waterside Inn, he brings a wealth of culinary experience to this rustic Knowstone venue. Grab a drink by the large inglenook fireplace, or sit beneath the pub's exquisite Renaissance style ceiling (you'll see what we mean when you arrive) and dine on affordably priced Michelin-star food.

Set your sat nav for the town of Bideford to find **Number Eight**. This award-winning restaurant is run solely by a talented couple called Joshua and Chloe. The ever changing and highly seasonal tasting menu showcases Joshua's culinary chops, while Chloe is on hand to provide guests with attentive service and a cracking drinks list. Be prepared to join a waiting list if you want to dine at Number Eight, because the last time we checked tables were being snapped up three months in advance.

Number Eight, William Reavell

MORE OF OUR FOODIE FAVOURITES

The Tytherleigh Arms, Axminster

Glebe House, Colyton

The Rusty Pig, Ottery St Mary

The Jack in the Green, Rockbeare

The Puffing Billy, Exton

Winslade Manor, nr Exeter

The Salty Monk, Sidford

Saveur, Exmouth

The Orange Tree, Torquay

Riverford Field Kitchen, Totnes

Paschoe House, Bow

Lewtrenchard Manor, Lewdown

Gidleigh Park, Chagford

Hotel Endsleigh, Dartmoor

The Old Inn, Dartmoor

The Cornish Arms, Tavistock

The Horn of Plenty, Tavistock

Pyne Arms, nr Barnstaple

The Grove Inn, Kings Nympton

The Antidote, Ilfracombe

Le Petit Bouchee, Witheridge

The Swan, Bampton

Maverick Loves

GAIA Skincare

When GAIA Skincare was founded in 2016, the brand was built on connections, experiences, and consideration for others. Its founders shared a vision of bringing a higher level of wellness to the spa industry through natural products and a holisitic approach to wellbeing. Today, 6 years since GAIA Skincare's journey began, this vision has blossomed into a reality...

Taking inspiration from Gaia, the ancient Greek goddess known as Mother Nature, it should come as no surprise that the roots of GAIA Skincare stem back to Ancient Greece and their natural approach to medicine. That's why each of their cruelty-free products is handmade using traditional methods, blending together the finest ingredients, plant actives and essential oils.

We first discovered GAIA Skincare through their flagship Gaia Spa at Boringdon Hall Hotel (p.16) where they offer a signature range of treatments, such as cystal therapy and restorative massage. We fell in love with their sumptuous range of skincare products, which features everything from balancing bath oils to nurturing body balms, as well as a new prenatal range to nuture and support expecting mums-to-be. Each of their products has been carefully blended to help melt away stresses, awaken our senses and offer a sense of calm and relaxation.

GAIA Skincare's holistic ethos doesn't end at what we put on our skin – they also care about our environment. That's why they opt for plastic-free packaging wherever possible, selling many of their products in glass bottles, along with creams and balms being sealed in biodegradable bamboo jars. They understand the importance of not just recycling but reusing pakaging, which is why they invite customers to return empty jars to stockists and offer a 20% discount on product refills.

Find out more at gaiaskincare.com and keep reading to discover four of our favourite GAIA Skincare products...

1

2

3

4

skincare favourites

We love these sumptuous **Gaia Skincare** products that allow us to bring their
luxurious spa experience into our homes...

1. Calming Bath Oil | £30, 100ml

Soothe your mind and body with this nurturing bath oil. Its calming blend of pure lavender, chamomile, and orange blossom essential oils are complemented by organic jojoba oil that's rich in vitamin E.

Why we love it: It leaves your skin feeling hydrated and soft and it's perfect for unwinding in the evening. Pour two capfuls of into a running bath and let the light aromas relax your mind and body.

2. Crystal Everglow Serum | £60, 15ml

This lightweight, rejuvenating serum helps promote a youthful glow to your skin. It's infused with rose quartz, but it's the hibiscus that gives this serum its warm pink glow. It's equipped with natural acids to purify skin and increase cell regeneration while providing anti-inflammatory and moisturising properties.

Why we love it: Natural quartz is abundant in minerals found at the earth's surface, so it infuses the serum with all the crystal benefits for more enhanced and effective results.

3. Crystal Purifying Mask | £38, 50g

GAIA's Crystal Purifying Mask combines the energy and healing properties of rose quartz crystal with the purest natural ingredients. Its deep pink colour is derived from pomegranate and hibiscus, which prevent damage to your skin and reduce the breakdown of collagen. It's a great source of vitamin C and encouraging cell rejuvenation.

Why we love it: It helps to prevent breakouts and it leaves your skin feeling refreshed, firm and smooth.

4. Awakening Body Scrub | £38, 240g

This clay and sea salt body scrub exfoliates, cleanses, and deeply moisturises your skin. Apply it to your body with long, firm sweeping strokes, paying special attention to areas of dry skin. Gentle buffing will help to improve circulation and remove dead skin cells, revealing smoother, healthier skin.

Why we love it: It's made with GAIA's signature awakening blend of rosemary, ravensara, peppermint, and lemongrass pure essential oils, so the fragrance is subtle but heavenly.

devon's

Independent Shopping

When visiting a new town nothing quite beats the joy of stumbling upon an indie shop after meandering up some promising yet higgledy-piggledy side streets. Thankfully, Devon is full of passionate people running independent businesses that breathe life into their towns and cities. Here are a few of our favourites...

In the seaside town of Seaton you'll find **Triptych Gallery**: a gallery and picture framing business with incredible taste in art and homewares. If you're anything like us, you'll be tempted inside by their fabulous window displays and stay for the affordable art and handmade wares. Featured makers include the likes of local illustrator, Linzi West, landscape painter, Debbie Lush, and the brilliant Gilliflower Pottery.

Situated in a quaint courtyard in Axminster is **The Courthouse Makers.** This charming shop showcases the work of over 60 modern British craftspeople and sells everything from hand-carved spoons to original paintings and ceramics. We love the fact that everything on sale is made by passionate makers and through purchasing a product you're supporting a creative person in growing their business.

Find ethical clothing store **Sancho's** on Exeter's thriving Fore Street. Owner Kalkidan Legesse knows her stuff when it comes to fashion and sustainability. Everything she sells has a conscience and is made in fair trade conditions with organic, recycled and regenerative materials. What's not to love?

Velvet & Parade, Honiton

Niaski Studio by @girl_behindthelens (also p.140)

Velvet and Parade is a family-run lifestyle store based in Honiton's popular Combe Garden Centre. We've been shopping with these lovely ladies since they first opened their doors and we always find the perfect gift amongst their curated selection of homeware and accessories. Their aim has always been to create a beautiful setting that brings joy to the everyday – an ethos that is echoed in their fabulous wares and warm service.

Cat lovers will adore Niaski in the sleepy seaside town of Budleigh Salterton. It's a colourful shop at 32 Fore Street that showcases the work of Devon artist, Nia Gould. Her vibrant illustrations put a feline twist on popular culture icons – think Pablo Picatso, Kitty Stardust, Frida Catlo – and her work is featured on a range of products from stationery and art prints, to pet collars and coffee table books.

Walking around **Bøde Living's** showroom in Sidmouth is like taking a lesson in contemporary design. There's a huge range of mood-lifting homewares and soft furnishings that will bring a touch of vibrancy to your home. In case it wasn't obvious from the name (Bøde is Danish) there's a real focus on Scandinavian design. But we also love the retro-chic aesthetic they have going on, from kitsch vases and candy striped cushions to retro inspired garden parasols.

Relish Home in Kingsbridge is run by husband and wife team, Amy and Shaun, who are skilled in both interior design and craftsmanship; talents they use to revive antiques and create bespoke interiors. Inside their beautiful shop you can expect a satisfying blend of modern and rustic home décor, and characterful pieces with lots of texture. Their main draw, if you're interested in sustainable living, is their lovingly restored reclaimed furniture.

With brick and mortar shops in Salcombe, Exeter, Totnes and Kingsbridge there's plenty of opportunities to pop into clothing and lifestyle store, **Busby & Fox** (pictured left). Each of their beautifully curated stores is brimming with evergreen pieces that are relaxed and versatile. Shop here for soft and sustainable wardrobe staples that layer well and stand the test of time.

Beautiful **The Forest and Co** on Totnes High Street sells all manner of homewares and accessories that we covet. Everything is comforting, elegant and understated, with a touch of eccentricity. We can't get enough of their luxurious patterned quilts, rustic tablewares and unique furniture items. If you're looking to stamp some personality onto your home, start here!

Head to **Will Bees Bespoke** in Salcombe for exquisitely made bags in all shapes and sizes. Their combined workshop and retail space on Island Street is a riot of colour and oozes sophistication. We love their signature collection, featuring queen bee-printed fabrics, as well as their new collection 'The Bee Garden' in collaboration with former Head of Design at Liberty Art Fabrics, Emma Mawston. Every piece features original designs inspired by the flora and bees native to Devon and Cornwall. Bee-autiful!

Sunshine & Snow by Stephanie Osmond

You can't miss colourful **Sunshine & Snow** on Bideford's Mill Street. Its vibrant, block colour shop front is the perfect advert for all the design-led homeware and artisanal gifts inside. The shop sells its own range of hand-picked vintage clothing (Sunshine Vintage) as well as unique décor, reclaimed furniture, and children's toys. There's also an onsite coffee bar that sells Origin Coffee and cakes from The Exploding Bakery.

Jo Allum Coastal Art & Homewares is a charming shop in the coastal resort of Woolacombe, where artist Jo Allum sells her original artwork and handmade homewares. Her work is inspired by the stretch of coastline she calls home, as well as surf culture and exotic travels. Her paintings and handmade lampshades are a fabulous way to infuse your home with the magic of the rugged North Devon coast.

Maverick Meets

Wanderlust Life

When Georgie Roberts set up jewellery brand Wanderlust Life nearly 10 years ago, she couldn't imagine that making and selling her pieces would become her full-time job. Today, she employs a team of 16 people from a studio and shop in Braunton, North Devon, and the brand releases two collections every year, each with their own themes and design styles. Here, Georgie tells us about her story so far...

I'd had lots of different jobs, from working with creative agencies to running yoga retreats. At one point working with Damien Hirst to open a gallery in Ilfracombe. But I realised none of these roles were really satisfying my needs. I knew I wanted to start my own business, and I loved travelling, so I took some inspiration from the places I've been to. I actually came up with the idea for Wanderlust Life when I was on a plane – I was doodling a kind of mind map of all the things I love doing. I knew I wanted the inspiration of travel to

be the impetus for something. When I got back to Devon, I started the business in my spare room while I was still working. It all started with one necklace that we still make today, and that's our signature fine cord necklace. Eventually I took a leap of faith and made it my full-time job!

My designs are often described as 'minimalistic' but I'm not sure I'd say that. I think it's more about the joy of stripping back the clutter from our lives. I love the pared-back aesthetic. There's a real beauty in the rawness of materials. It all started with our fine cord necklace, which is just a gemstone on a cord that you can barely see when it's worn. What everyone seems to love about it is it's so pared back and simple, but there's real strength in it from a design sense. That's one of our brand values that we've held onto over the years: we try to keep our pieces simple and stripped back.

It was when I had three or four people working with me on Wanderlust Life out of my house that we realised we needed more space. We found a shop in Ilfracombe that we originally used as a studio, but then we decided to open the doors and see if we got any customers. That was the point when we realised there was absolutely something in the hybrid shop/studio environment. It's a totally different retail experience. People love coming in and picking out their gemstones and seeing the jewellery being made in front of them. So, then we decided we needed even more space and found the shop we're in now in Braunton. It's a lovely small town and we have a lot more footfall because we're on the route to Saunton and Croyde. We haven't looked back!

The shop is a hybrid of Scandinavian and Japanese inspired design. We only wanted to use a few core materials, so we used lots of plywood and ash wood to keep it very stripped back just like our jewellery. We wanted to let the jewellery speak for itself. We have double-aspect windows, so we get a lot of natural light, which is important for showing off the gold and the gemstones in our pieces. A lot of people say they find it really calming and chilled out.

Our fine cord necklaces are firm favourites with our customers. It's easy to make them individual because they come in around 30 different gemstones and each one has its own properties that we've translated into a mantra. They're quite affordable, so it's nice to be able to offer something that can be so unique to an individual. It's almost like a storytelling piece. Our birth stone collection is also really popular. We collaborate with an artist down in Cornwall named Clara Jonas, who brings our mantras for each month to life with illustrations. One of the things people love about that collection is the way it's packaged. Each piece comes on a card designed by Clara which has the mantra and the meaning of the stone on it. It's almost like a little tarot card.

There are a few pieces in our summer collection that I'm really excited about. The theme is Revival, and we took a lot of inspiration from rummaging through old jewellery boxes. I also love our nexus rings. They're cast from a shell I picked up in Indonesia about 15 years ago. They're plain solid gold rings but they have quite an organic shape to them, they're kind of undulating on the surface. They have a really happy memory attached to them, so I love wearing them.

"Our jewellery can be worn as a kind of talisman and a reminder of what's possible within us."

Being a small business owner is all about having the right people around you. I'm really lucky that I've got a great team that are very supportive and collaborative. Everyone on our team is a vital part of what we do. There's usually seven or eight of us in the studio at one time, so depending on whoever gets to Spotify first we've usually got a really eclectic mix of music genres playing in the sudio. When Friday afternoon comes around don't be surprised if you hear some classic power ballads playing. We're always up for a bit of cheese and it helps everyone get psyched for the weekend.

There are lots of amazing creatives here in the southwest. I follow quite a few photographers online and we're working with one of them for our latest collection. Her business is called Travel & The Girls; she's a photographer named Louise Roberston based in Cornwall. I really like a clothing brand called Marazul run by Harri, who's also created a collective called Holan which does some really interesting stuff. Cornwall has a quite strong creative culture, but I think it can sometimes be a bit more challenging for new businesses up here in North Devon.

Despite its remoteness, I love the scenery and how rugged North Devon is. I grew up in Braunton so I was lucky to be so close to the sea. I feel very connected to the coastline, but I also really love the community. We've got an amazing, tight network of people here. You can be in the most beautiful place, but I think it's the community that brings everything together and makes a place truly beautiful.

Wanderlust Life, 14 Caen Street,
Braunton, Devon EX33 1AA
wanderlustlife.co.uk

devon's
Best Beaches

In a pretty nook of the South Hams coastline lies **Hope Cove and Thurlestone**, which are home to a charming collection of pubs and thatched cottages that hug two beautiful sandy beaches. It's also a great place to refuel after a walk along the South West Coast Path or a chilly dip in the sea. Strong swimmers can start at Inner Hope and end at Outer Hope, swimming around a headland and between the bays.

You can catch some gorgeous, soft sunsets from **Westward Ho! Beach** thanks to the wide-open skies along its extensive stretch of sand. Surf-wise, the beach is beginner friendly with a hire shop in the town, but if the bracing waves of the Atlantic aren't for you there's also a sea pool for a gentle dip. Alternatively, follow the coast round to Appledore: a charming fishing village on the River Torridge.

East Portlemouth Beach is a smooth sandy beach with clear waters and a relaxed feel, making it perfect for sunbathing and a quiet dip. From its golden shore you can admire the white houses of Salcombe, the boats bobbing in the estuary and the curve of sweeping green cliffs that keep the sands relatively sheltered. The easiest way to get to East Portlemouth is by ferry from Salcombe, to avoid narrow roads and full car parks. Once you're on the beach, find a quiet cove that catches the sunset.

Broad Sands Beach is North Devon's worst kept secret. Secluded by wild cliffs that are thick with luscious greenery, the beach opens to a stunning view of turquoise water. On a sunny day it has a, dare I say, tropical feel, but it's a shingle beach so don't expect golden sands!

Croyde Beach is one of North Devon's most popular beaches, with its fine golden sands and even finer surf. Surrounded by sand dunes and green rolling hills, this laidback beach is perfect for families and surfers alike. Croyde Village is just a short distance away, so when you're done on the beach you can head for a pint at one of its popular local pubs.

Blackpool Sands is a Blue Flag award-winning beach, backed by lush rolling hills, evergreens and scented pines. Despite its deceptive name, it's a shingle beach, named after the local town of Blackpool (near Dartmouth). Located in a sheltered bay, the beach is privately managed and kept in immaculate condition. It even boasts its own Café 'Venus Beach', where you can enjoy peaceful breakfasts and light lunches with some stunning sea views.

Cellars Beach is a little cove off the River Yealm. You can park at Noss Mayo and embark on the 35 minute trundle through pretty riverside woodland down to the beach. If the tide is high, the beach is reduced to a large rock, surrounded by see-to-the-bottom water - great for a cool plunge before drying off like a lizard in the sun. It's important to check the tide times though, as water can creep into part of the car park at high tide.

Ladram Bay is a beautifully curving pebble beach to the east of Budleigh Salterton, characterised by its dramatic, red sea stacks. It's fun to kayak or swim out to these sandstone islands, weave around them, discover caves to climb through and ledges to clamber on, or simply to see these wonderful towers from a different perspective.

The epitome of unspoilt rugged beauty, **Lannacombe Beach** feels wild but has soft sand. It's a quieter beach, tucked away and bordered by rock formations that reveal seaweed pools to explore when the tide goes out. This is a peaceful part of South Devon's coastline that welcomes dogs all year round.

Hartland Quay is known for its remarkable scenery, often featuring crashing waves, but always with towering cliffs and giant italic rock formations that jut into the sea. As you walk down from the top of the headland, there are far-reaching views of the North Devon coastline and on a good day you can surf and bathe against its dramatic backdrop.

Maverick Meets

Ella Slade

Photography by Girl Behind The Lens

"I've always wanted to be an artist," says 24-year-old painter Ella Slade. "My parents are incredibly supportive of this path and they've never had any objections to me pursuing art as a career. That support really helped me realise what I wanted to do."

In 2019, at just 22 years of age, Ella Slade opened her first studio and gallery space on Exmouth's state-of-the-art Sideshore Development. Ella's Studio is a first of its kind for the East Devon arts scene, which has largely been dominated by traditional landscape artists. Her work offers a fresh take on the classic seascape, injecting a much-needed sense of youth and vitality.

Growing up, Ella showed all the early signs of being a creative child, whether she was busy in the kitchen making apple pies or lacing flower fairies in the garden. When the rest of her class had their heads buried in their textbooks, Ella was skipping class to seek out the art rooms and get ahead on her sketchbooks.

"It's funny," she reflects. "I always remember painting a portrait of my mum when I was in year two. I painted her with a striped polo neck jumper and stiff arms that jutted out to either side. My mum laughed when she saw it, because she was just this square shape, but I still remember the joy of painting it and taking it home. She still has it hanging on the wall now!"

Ella's penchant for art and a childhood diagnosis of dyslexia led her on a less than conventional path. Passing on A-levels, she opted to study for a UAL Extended Diploma before attending Manchester School of Art. Strangely enough, it was during this period spent in northern England that she rekindled her love of the great outdoors and ignited a newfound passion for illustration.

"I did loads of illustrations at university, mainly based on the county of Devon and the things that influenced my childhood," she says. "I like depicting things in nature

because it's very comparative for people to look at. People from this part of the world can share in those childhood memories of going to the beach and picking up shells or finding a snail at the bottom of the garden".

Shortly after graduating Ella found herself immersed back in the landscapes she had imagined through her illustrations, though not in a way she could ever have predicted. "Lockdown restrictions were announced shortly after I graduated and I found myself unable to leave Devon," she explains. "This pulled me back into the roots of what I was originally doing and made me realise I wanted to pursue my art full time."

As UK lockdown came into full swing, it became clear that international travel was off the cards. So, Ella threw caution to the wind and decided to invest her travelling savings into opening her Exmouth studio. Conscious of her environmental impact, she was drawn to the Sideshore complex for its eco-credentials and its proximity to the sea. "I love the fact that all the buildings are sustainable," she explains.

"There's this natural vibe to the complex thanks the cedar cladding and its commitment to showcasing locally-grown businesses. I knew I'd be able to outfit my studio on a small budget and I could use reclaimed and recycled materials to bring it all together."

Ella utilised her family and friends to deck out the studio using up-cycled and repurposed materials. Recycled scaffolding boards, vintage ladders and reupholstered furniture are used to enhance the studio to great effect. "It's such an effortless way of designing a space, but those recycled elements make [the studio] a bit more interesting for people to look at. It proves that you don't always have to buy things new — you can and you should reuse furniture and objects."

With the studio established, the next challenge was to fill the space. Selling her art to the public was effectively a leap into uncharted territory, so Ella made the decision to source items from local makers and establish a small shop within the studio. Selling handpicked, local wares out front, she has filled her shelves with everything from delicate sea glass jewellery to recycled notebooks. There's also limited-edition placemats, printed

"I want to show the movement of the water and the character of the people or boats that inhabit my paintings."

director chairs, and lampshades featuring her work. Meanwhile, the back of the shop serves as a private studio space, where Ella can apply her newfound illustrative skills to the coastal vistas of Devon. "When I first starting painting seascapes, they were all abstract. But as my journey and my style of painting has developed, I feel like I've become a little bit more literal. I started pouring the skills I learned at university into my paintings, and it gives them more character and helps me to tell a story through them. Devon has always been quite stuck in this traditional way of working and painting. I have no issue with those kinds of paintings, but I'd like to think of my work as being slightly out of the box and a little bit more playful."

It's this fusion of the abstract and realism that gives Ella's paintings a unique form of energy. Each of the characters who inhabit her paintings have a little life of their own. They invoke a sense of nostalgia, and you get the sense that Ella wants the observer to connect to her seascapes on a level beyond pretty seaside views.

"I want the viewer to immerse themselves in my work," she says. "Especially my aerial view paintings. I've been told that those give people an airy feel. It's like they're in some sort of dreamland, because when they look from above it's such an unknown sort of perspective. It's the same with waves. That dramatised movement in the waves, the water being peeled up and bubbles foaming – you can almost hear that movement when you see it on a canvas. Whether it's a voluminous barrel wave crashing into shore or the soft, gentle surf – I want the viewers to feel immersed in the scenes."

Like many of the artists I've interviewed before, Ella Slade trusts her intuition in the creative process. "I tend to layer acrylic paint onto canvas or recycled plywood" she explains. "It lets me build up the painting and give it a tactile quality. I often use palette knives and brushes, but sometimes I introduce my hands. I start by

separating the sky from the sea, but from here I tend to get a lot looser before I tie myself up with the details. It gives a painting more energy."

When it comes to real life coastlines, Ella admits that it's Devon's north coast that provides a constant source of inspiration. "My partner and I like to make spontaneous trips to North Devon in his van. The waves up there are awesome and there's an energy to the place. You're hit with this sense of escapism and you come away feeling fresh and rejuvenated."

But for all the beauty and inspiration of North Devon, it's Ella's hope that East Devon will emerge as a new creative hub for young people. "There's such a drive and market for art down in Cornwall, but there isn't enough happening for the contemporary art scene in East Devon," she says. "There aren't enough places that will highlight the work of young or aspiring artists who may not have cracked the competitive art world yet. It's something I'm keen to explore in the future – so watch this space!"

Follow Ella online at ellasdevon.com
Or visit her studio in person at
Ella's Sideshore, Exmouth EX8 2GD

Notes